FIELD GUIDE TO

BACKYARD BIRDS OF THE MIDWEST

First published in 2008 by Cool Springs Press, an imprint of the Quayside
Publishing Group, P.O. Box 2828, Brentwood, TN 37024 USA.

Photographs of the American Tree Sparrow and American Woodcook
courtesy of Jupiter Images. All other photographs provided by Brian E.
Small.

Cool Springs Press titles are also available at discounts in bulk quantity
for industrial or sales-promotional use. For details write to Special Sales
Manager at Cool Springs Press, P.O. Box 2828, Brentwood, TN 37024
USA.

To find out more about our books, visit us online at
www.coolspringspress.com.

ISBN-13: 978-1-59186-007-5

7 8 9 10 11 12

Project Manager: Ashley Hubert
Art Director: Marc Pewitt
Production: Publication Services, Inc.
Illustrator: Publication Services, Inc.

Printed in the United States of America

FIELD GUIDE TO

BACKYARD BIRDS OF THE
MIDWEST

COOL
SPRINGS
PRESS

FRANKLIN, TENNESSEE

CONTENTS

From sweeping sand dunes to dense coniferous forest, thousands of miles of lake-shore, tallgrass prairies, and teeming marshes, the Midwest boasts an array of unique habitats that are home to a wide variety of birds. An abundance of forests and freshwater sources make this area the preferred migration path for hundreds of birds, and others make it their home year-round.

The Midwest was once blanketed in grassland prairies and vast woodlands. But with the expansion of suburbs and large-scale farming, the preferred habitats of many birds disappeared. Today, national organizations and local societies establish and maintain prairie and wetland conservation areas and forest preserves in an attempt to boost dwindling bird populations. Approximately 500 species appear regularly in the region, and the range maps in this guide will help you identify the birds you see in your area.

If you are new to birding, a few basic strategies will increase the likelihood of spotting and identifying local species. The first step is to obtain at least one useful field guide. Carry it with you in the field, and keep it on hand for easy use. When you sight an unfamiliar bird, watch its behavior, note its coloring and unique field marks, and then consult your guide to confirm its name.

The second item to keep handy near your observation window is a pair of binoculars. A quality pair can often be purchased for under $100, and 7x or 8x magnification is ideal.

Learning to recognize bird songs is another valuable investment. Audio CDs and online resources provide samples of hundreds of common bird calls and songs, and knowing the sounds of your common backyard residents will make it easier to recognize an uncommon visitor.

Consider joining a local birding club. These organizations frequently organize birding walks and field trips, where more experienced birders can answer your questions, help you identify unfamiliar species, and recommend the best local bird-watching sites.

The simplest way to begin birding is to watch the birds in your own backyard. Even a small yard with one or two feeders can be home to dozens of birds. Some affordable options for seed-eaters include black-oil sunflower seeds, white millet, peanuts, mixed seed, cracked corn, and thistle seed. Insectivores may be happily

Baltimore Oriole

at home among garden trees and shrubbery, but in winter, many turn to berries and suet cakes. Others are drawn to flowering plants.

Learning the dietary preferences of your favorite species can help you decide how best to draw them to your property. Bird boxes for cavity-nesting species are another easy way to intimately observe their behavior. Whether you encounter feathered friends close to home or far afield, birding is sure to become an exciting and rewarding hobby.

House Finch

I n 1940, New York City pet shops began to sell California's native house finches as pet songbirds. In the ensuing crackdown on this practice, a small population of the brightly plumed birds was released. They eventually spread to suburban communities throughout the Midwest.

Description
Similar to the purple finch of the North and West, the 6-inch male is brown above with a red brow, bib, and rump. The female, identified by a white eyebrow, and juvenile are paler with streaked bellies.

Preferred Habitat
Now widespread and common in both the East and the West, the house finch competes with the house sparrow for nesting sites and food in cities, towns, and farming areas.

Feeding Habits
Finches are common visitors to backyard seed feeding stations, and otherwise survive on fruit, bread crumbs, berries, buds, and flower parts.

Migration Habits
The introduced eastern population has thrived and spread across the continent, now separated from the native western population by less than 100 miles.

Placement of Feeders
While these welcome visitors are perched on your mixed seed feeder, try to distinguish the female house finch from the female house sparrow. Also, watch for finch nests in your hanging flower baskets or ornamental garden trees.

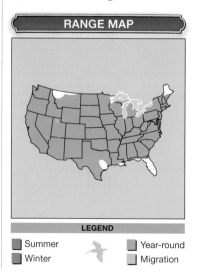

RANGE MAP

LEGEND

Summer Year-round
Winter Migration

Unusual among birds, cardinals mate for life and stay paired year-round. The colorful pair sings in duets, completing each other's loud whistled phrases *what cheer, cheer, cheer* or *sweet-sweet-sweet-sweet*. The male may act aggressively toward the female at a feeding station, but she continues feeding, undisturbed.

Description
Named for the robes of Catholic cardinals, the male's bright red plumage and black face are unmistakable. Females are grayish brown with red highlights on the crest, wings, and tail, and an orange-red bill. Both measure 7.5–9 inches long.

Preferred Habitat
Common in gardens, parks, thickets, woodlands, and hedgerows, cardinals nest in a shrub or a tangle of vines.

red

Males feed the first brood while the female starts a second, with up to four broods each year.

Feeding Habits
Cardinals have a varied diet encompassing weed seeds, wild fruit, insects, grains, and even maple syrup from woodpecker holes.

Migration Habits
These nonmigrants are less territorial in winter, joining with small flocks. In recent decades their range has extended farther north.

Placement of Feeders
This frequent feeder visitor uses its short, conical bill to crack open seeds, especially sunflower seeds, safflower seeds, and cracked corn.

RANGE MAP

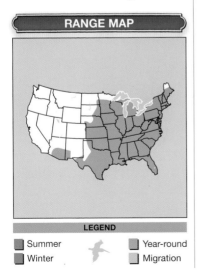

LEGEND

Summer   Year-round
Winter   Migration

Pileated Woodpecker

Among North American woodpeckers, the pileated is second in size only to the ivory-billed, which was thought extinct until 2005. Nicknamed the "logcock," the pileated species is a magnificent red-crested bird that can strip sheets of bark and chisel huge holes in decaying trees.

Description

Crow sized at 16–19 inches, the bird is black above and below, with a red crest, black-and-white striped face, white stripes down the neck, and white underwings. The male has a red mustache while the female has a black mustache and a shorter red crest.

Preferred Habitat

These woodpeckers prefer mature deciduous woodlands, but with the clearing of many forests they have adapted to younger trees and abandoned farmland. Both parents share the responsibility of incubating the young, raised in a cavity of a dead trunk or a high limb.

Feeding Habits

Like other woodpeckers these birds pry grubs, carpenter ants, and wood-borers from tree bark, also consuming acorns, berries, and nuts.

Migration Habits

This widespread species is a year-round resident of the East, the Midwest, and the West from Washington to California.

Placement of Feeders

It is not uncommon to see these forest birds or hear their fast, laughing *yucka-yucka-yucka* calls. They occasionally visit suet feeders along forest edges.

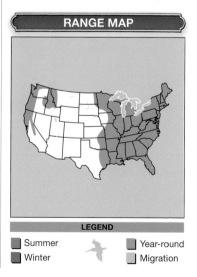

RANGE MAP

LEGEND

| ■ Summer | ■ Year-round |
| ■ Winter | ■ Migration |

Although less common than the pine siskin, the tame and approachable pine grosbeak is the largest finch of the Midwest, where it is often seen eating small grains of sand to aid in digestion, or bathing in fluffy fresh snow.

Description

This large, stubby finch measures 8–10 inches, with a curved bill. The rosy male has dark streaks on his back, dark wings with two white bars, and a long notched tail. The female has a gray body with a dull yellow head and rump.

Preferred Habitat

During nesting season, brushy clearings in coniferous forests are preferred, but deciduous forests provide a substantial portion of the bird's seed diet.

RANGE MAP

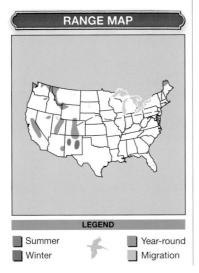

LEGEND

- Summer
- Winter
- Year-round
- Migration

Feeding Habits

Regular travel is required as the grosbeak harvests the seeds and fruit of mountain ash and cedar trees. Insects supplement its diet in summer.

Migration Habits

Wintering south to the Dakotas, these northern birds breed from the Pacific Northwest south to the Desert Southwest.

Placement of Feeders

Although migrant populations vary from year to year, grosbeaks are occasional backyard visitors during migration. Distinguish the female from female purple finches or house finches by her large size.

Red-bellied Woodpecker

A bristly layer of feathers protects the nostrils from wood dust as the woodpecker hammers out a rapid message on a utility pole. This sturdy bird is equipped for a lifetime of climbing and drilling, bracing itself upright with a stiff tail and using its long toes to grip its perch.

Description
The 10-inch woodpecker is stout and strong, ladder-barred black and white above with a tan face and underparts. Males have a characteristic red crown and nape, while females have a red nape only.

Preferred Habitat
Any orchard, park, farmland, or open swampy woodland with a handful of dead trees might be home to the red-bellied, which bores a nest hole in dead tree trunks or utility poles.

Feeding Habits
Its stiff bill chips away bark to find insects, wood-boring beetles, seeds, and wild fruits. Its long, cylindrical tongue has a hard tip to spear insects and a sticky coating to lap up ants.

Migration Habits
Found in the East and Midwest, northernmost birds may migrate south in winter, where they are common in parks and southeastern woodlands.

Placement of Feeders
Listen for the woodpecker's low, hoarse rattling call. In winter they turn to feeders, and those wintering in Florida suck juice from oranges.

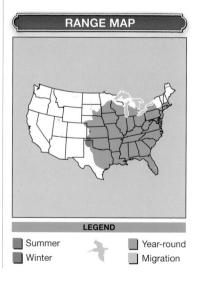

RANGE MAP

LEGEND

Summer   Year-round

Winter   Migration

From his perch on a swaying cattail, the male blackbird sings his gurgled song while flashing his red shoulder patches, eagerly establishing his mating territory before the females arrive.

Description

This large blackbird, 7–9.5 inches, is common and unmistakable. The black male has bright red patches on the shoulders, bordered by a yellow band. Females and juveniles are heavily streaked with brown and lack the red patches.

Preferred Habitat

Perhaps most common in marshes, swamps, and wet meadows, this marsh bird will nest near any body of water, including dry pastures, farmland, and roadside ditches. Breeding birds construct a new nest of marsh reeds for each of the season's two or three broods.

Feeding Habits

Seeds provide the blackbird's main sustenance in spring and autumn, but it switches to insects for the summer season.

Migration Habits

While their extensive breeding range stretches from Washington to Maine, these birds winter across most of the United States, but can be found year-round throughout the Midwest.

Placement of Feeders

The flashy red-wing is a familiar sight in backyards and parks across the country, particularly when they join up with other blackbirds for autumn and winter feeding in mobs of hundreds of thousands or even millions.

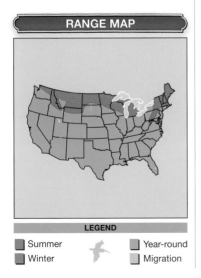

RANGE MAP

LEGEND

■ Summer ■ Year-round
■ Winter ■ Migration

Alder Flycatcher

brown

Until the 1970s, the alder flycatcher and the willow flycatcher were thought to be a single species, known as Traill's flycatcher. These two birds are identical in appearance, so the alder flycatcher is best distinguished from its relative by its distinctive *fee-bee-o* call.

Description

At 6 inches long, this backyard bird displays an olive-brown head and back, two dull whitish wing bars, and a pale olive breast. Unlike many young birds, the alder flycatcher knows its *fee-bee-o* call from birth.

Preferred Habitat

Named for its thicket of choice, it can be found in dense alder, willow, or dogwood thickets, usually near streams, lakes, or swamps. They nest in dense bushes or shrubs.

Feeding Habits

From its perch on a branch or high-wire, beetles, moths, wasps, and other flying insects are an easy catch. It will also eat aphids, caterpillars, or spiders from foliage.

Migration Habits

From mid-May to mid-June, the alder flycatcher migrates from the tropics northward, and reverses the journey from mid-August through September.

Placement of Feeders

If dense thickets and a water source are available, these birds can be drawn to a feeder of berries and seeds.

RANGE MAP

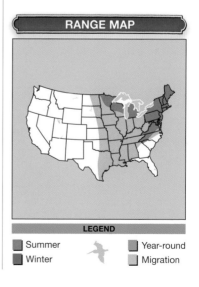

LEGEND

■ Summer   ■ Year-round
■ Winter   ■ Migration

This master of disguise is so well camouflaged that birders may walk right past without noticing him. Sitting silently with its bill turned straight up to the sky, the bittern can take on the appearance of a tree stump, a root, or a dead limb, or it can sway back and forth to blend in perfectly with its reedy home.

Description

The pear-shaped bittern ranges from 24–34 inches long, streaked dark brown above, with dark wingtips and yellow legs and feet. Its white throat has long, reddish brown stripes.

Preferred Habitat

In secretive, isolated pairs the bitterns build a reed platform nest near the water's edge in marshes, fens, grassy lakeshores, or wet meadows.

brown

Feeding Habits

Standing in the shallow water, the bittern waits in perfect stillness until a hapless fish draws near, then it plunges its stiff beak into the water to stab its meal. Insects, frogs, crayfish, reptiles, eels, and water snakes are common prey.

Migration Habits

This water-loving bird breeds throughout the northern half of the United States but can be found in the summer throughout the Upper Midwest.

Placement of Feeders

In March and April, the usually solitary, silent males make brief public courtship displays. Between dusk and midnight, listen for a low-pitched *oonk-a-lunk* call.

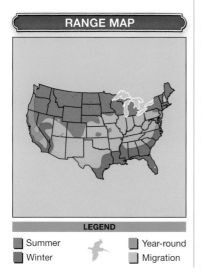

RANGE MAP

LEGEND

- Summer
- Winter
- Year-round
- Migration

American Golden Plover

brown

This small bird, only 10 inches long, makes an incredible journey each spring and autumn of nearly 10,000 miles over the Atlantic between Canada and South America, or over the Pacific to Australia for its well-deserved winter rest.

Description
Spring adults are mottled black flecked with gold above and below, with a white S-shaped stripe from the crown to the shoulders. By autumn they molt into whitish underparts, with less gold above and a paler eyebrow.

Preferred Habitat
During spring migration the birds rest in agricultural fields on their way to their breeding grounds in the tundra of northern Canada and Alaska. During autumn migration they prefer mud flats and sod farms.

Feeding Habits
Plovers consume mainly insects, mollusks, and crustaceans, but often fatten up on crowberries before their long journey.

Migration Habits
Flocks of 500 to 5,000 pass through the central United States and the Midwest during spring migration In autumn, much smaller flocks cruise along the Atlantic Coast.

Placement of Feeders
Watch for tired birds riding the winds or resting in wet crop fields during migration periods. Plovers are now federally protected and their populations are bouncing back.

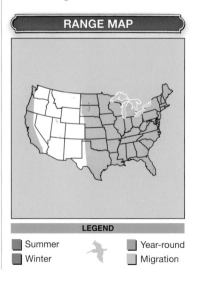

RANGE MAP

LEGEND
■ Summer   ■ Year-round
■ Winter   ■ Migration

This sparrow spends its life in brushy plains and southern Arctic tundra where the few trees are scraggly and weather-worn. The hardy tree sparrow consumes more seeds than almost any other sparrow, eating a quarter of its weight in weed seeds every day.

Description

Best identified by the black spot in the center of its tan breast, the streaky brown adults measure up to 6.5 inches long, with a chestnut crown and two white wing bars. The two-tone bill is dark above and yellow below.

Preferred Habitat

Arctic thickets, brushy fields, and marshes are the tree sparrow's ideal home. Their ground nests are lined with fur plucked from lemmings, a

common Arctic rodent.

Feeding Habits

Seeds, berries, and catkins make up the tree sparrow's diet for most of the year, supplemented by insects and spiders in summer.

Migration Habits

Traveling in flocks of up to 200, the tree sparrow leaves its wintering grounds across the inland states in early March to head north.

Placement of Feeders

Backyard feeders are familiar haunts to this common winter bird, but also look for foraging flocks pecking in frozen fields and weedy prairies, singing merrily.

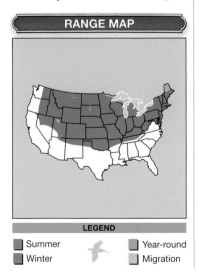

RANGE MAP

LEGEND

Summer

Winter

Year-round

Migration

brown

American Woodcock

During spring courtship, the male woodcock gives a fascinating display. After sunset, and sometimes all night long, he parades around his territory buzzing like an insect, then leaps into flight crooning a warbling song, then dives in zigzags back to the ground.

Description
Stocky and large-headed, the 11.5-inch woodcock is mottled brown with a camouflage leaf pattern above and rust or buff below. The bill is very long, and the eyes are set far back beneath a black-barred crown.

Preferred Habitat
Woodcocks raise their broods in brushy fields, moist thickets, or damp woodlands. After breeding season, they relocate to marshes, wetlands, and swamps.

Feeding Habits
In 24 hours a woodcock can eat its weight in earthworms, plucking them out of the loose earth with its long bill. They also consume insects, berries, and the seeds of some grasses and weeds.

Migration Habits
This early migrant nests long before the spring's final frosts. They are found in the East and the Midwest, breeding in the North and wintering in the southern half of their range.

Placement of Feeders
From mid-March to June, but especially in April, listen for the male's sensational courting song, or their common *peent* call.

RANGE MAP

LEGEND

Summer   Year-round
Winter   Migration

Barred Owl

In the resounding darkness of the deep woods at night, a chilling call rings out—*Who cooks for-you, who cooks for you-all?* The nocturnal barred owl is a varied vocalist, with calls that include hoots, howls, barks, and squawks.

Description

At 18-24 inches, this squat owl is twice the size of the eastern screech-owl, and females are slightly larger. Its ruffled plumage is brown above and pale below, with dark horizontal barring across its chest, vertical streaks on the belly, and white barring down its back.

Preferred Habitat

In dense woodlands, river valleys, or swamps, females lay eggs on the bare floor of a tree cavity, in a simple wooden nest box, or in an abandoned hawk's nest.

brown

RANGE MAP

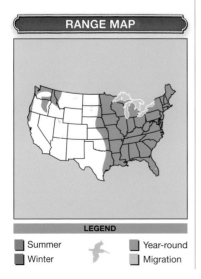

LEGEND

- Summer
- Winter
- Year-round
- Migration

Feeding Habits

Although primarily nocturnal, the barred species is often seen hunting during daylight, seeking mice, frogs, snakes, insects, rodents, small owls or birds, and crayfish.

Migration Habits

Owls are common year-round in the East and Midwest, and along the Pacific Coast to California.

Placement of Feeders

On overcast afternoons, their unique calls can lead you straight to their roosts, where they are calm and tame. Also try imitating their simpler calls to lure them near.

Bay-breasted Warbler

brown

This warbler's population fluctuates in relation to cyclical infestations of spruce budworms, pests that devastate spruce forests. In infestation years, there may be up to six times as many bay-breasted warblers.

Description
Measuring 5–6 inches long, breeding males have chestnut on the crown, throat, and sides, with a black face and forehead, a pale ear patch and buff underparts. Females are similar but lack the side patches. Nonbreeding males are dull green with buff sides.

Preferred Habitat
In spruce forests across Canada, the bird builds a bulky cup of twigs, bark, and grass in a conifer. During budworm years, females lay two additional eggs.

Feeding Habits
To minimize competition with other warblers, this bird scours mid-level branches for caterpillars, spiders, flies, budworms, and insect larvae. In their wintering grounds in South America, they eat mostly fruit.

Migration Habits
In summer they are found in parts of the Upper Midwest and New England. In winter they cross the continent on the way to Panama and Colombia.

Placement of Feeders
Watch for this common migrant from May to June, when they are easy to identify, but once they drop their breeding plumage, males look very similar to blackpoll warblers.

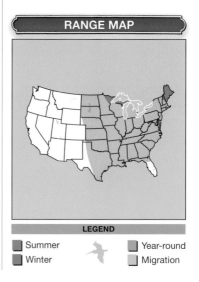

RANGE MAP

LEGEND

■ Summer ■ Year-round
■ Winter ■ Migration

Just before dawn, while a female songbird is away from her nest, an intruder rolls an egg out of the nest and replaces it with her own. The imposter fledgling will dominate the other chicks until it grows to maturity and rejoins its original species, the brown-headed cowbird. Often vilified as a brood parasite, the female cowbird leaves more than 20 eggs each season in the nests of more than 200 other species.

Description

The 6–8 inch glossy black male has a brown head, while the female is grayish brown overall. Both issue a *check* or rattling call.

Preferred Habitat

Once found only in the Great Plains, where it followed roaming buffalo herds, the brown-headed cowbird has thrived on suburbanization and is today found from coast to coast, favoring woodland edges, thickets, roadsides, and towns.

RANGE MAP

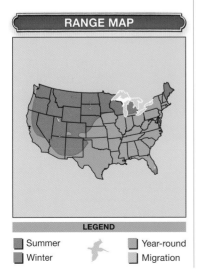

LEGEND

- Summer
- Winter
- Year-round
- Migration

Feeding Habits

Alongside other blackbirds and starlings, the cowbird forages on the ground for insects, seeds, and grains. Grasshoppers are a particular favorite.

Migration Habits

These birds are found year-round in the Northeast, Midwest, and along the entire West Coast.

Placement of Feeders

This bird is drawn to grains, seeds, berries, cracked corn, or sunflower hearts.

Carolina Wren

S witching without pause from *wheat-eater, wheat-eater, wheat!* to *tweedle, tweedle* or *tea kettle, tea kettle,* the Carolina wren sings up to 40 different songs all day long, regardless of season.

Description
Although similar to the house wren, the Carolina wren can be identified by its upturned tail. Measuring 6 inches, the bird is mainly reddish-brown with a white eyebrow swash, white chin, and buff underparts.

Preferred Habitat
Found in woodlands, thickets, undergrowth near water, and garden shrubs, the wren constructs small nests of grass, stems, and bark in a tree cavity or man-made object.

Feeding Habits
Flitting from plant to plant, these omnivores eat primarily insects and other small animals, as well as fruit and seeds.

Migration Habits
Carolina wrens inhabit the Northeast and Midwest year-round, never migrating, which means that a harsh winter can devastate populations. But young birds seem to expand northward after mild winters. They mate long term, staying paired year-round.

Placement of Feeders
As the only wren to frequent garden feeders, these cheery singers are drawn to fruit and suet, peanut butter, sunflower seeds, and nuts. They will often nest in birdhouses or other man-made objects, such as baskets, mailboxes, stone walls, or tin cans.

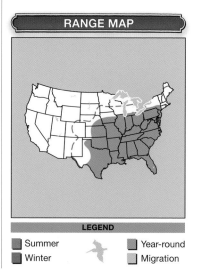

RANGE MAP

LEGEND

■ Summer ■ Year-round
■ Winter   ■ Migration

brown

These sleek, elegant birds are highly social, often seen lined up on a wire or branch passing berries or flower petals from one bird to the next. Best identified by a narrow, black "bandit" mask across the eyes, the crested bird has yellow tail tips and waxy red tips on the inner wing feathers.

Description

The 8-inch waxwing's plumage is a beautiful blend of soft pastel browns and grays above and below.

Preferred Habitat

Waxwings enjoy the close company of their own kind, making them one of the few songbirds to nest in colonies. They build bulky twig nests in open woodlands, orchards, gardens, and parks.

Feeding Habits

The bird consumes mainly berries and flower buds from berry-bearing trees and shrubs, especially cedar cones. Overripe, fermenting berries cause temporary intoxication, a startling sight for observant birders. During summer they also catch insects.

Migration Habits

This stunning species breeds across the northern half of the United States wintering in the lower states from the East Coast to the West Coast.

Placement of Feeders

Announcing their arrival with a high-pitched whistle, small winter flocks frequently descend on parks and gardens in search of cedar and rowan berries.

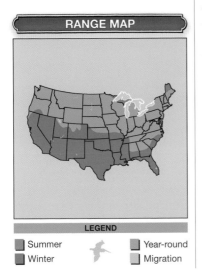

RANGE MAP

LEGEND

■ Summer
■ Winter
■ Year-round
■ Migration

brown

Chimney Swift

brown

Long ago abandoning its traditional habitat, the chimney swift selected the hollow towers accompanying human settlements for its home, both in nesting season and during migration. At sundown swarms of these fast flyers funnel like a tornado into large chimneys.

Description
Shaped like a boomerang in flight, the 5.5-inch swift is one of the world's fastest flying birds. Adult birds are dark gray-brown all over, with a short, stubby tail and long, narrow, curved wings.

Preferred Habitat
This species is found in all habitats across the East. Adults use saliva to glue a twig nest onto a vertical wall within a chimney, barn, well, or tree cavity. A second male often assists with raising the fledglings.

Feeding Habits
The swift spends its life on the wing, swallowing insects whole as it flies and dipping into rivers and streams to drink and bathe.

Migration Habits
These birds breed from the Great Plains east to the coast, traveling to South America in September.

Placement of Feeders
Large flocks return to favorite chimney sites year after year. In place of suitable chimneys, specially designed towers can be erected to draw flocks to your own property.

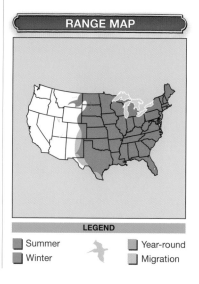

RANGE MAP

LEGEND

Summer	Year-round
Winter	Migration

I ronically classified as a songbird because it shares with those species a special resonating voice box, the grackle is known for its piercing, high-pitched screech. Its harsh call is reflected in its name, derived from the Latin *graculous* meaning "to cough."

Description

A large bird measuring up to 12.5 inches, the grackle has a long, wedge-shaped tail and yellow eyes. Males appear iridescent bronze or black with purple, greenish, or bronze highlights, while the female is less glossy and shorter tailed.

Preferred Habitat

Grackles are common in groves, towns, farmland, marshes, thickets, or suburban landscapes, where food is plentiful.

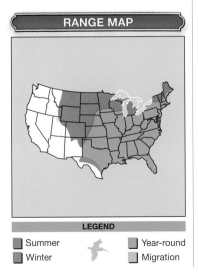

RANGE MAP

LEGEND

- ■ Summer
- ■ Winter
- ■ Year-round
- ■ Migration

brown

Feeding Habits

Scanning the ground, scouring trees or shrubs, or wading in water, this blackbird seeks insects, seeds, fruit, grain, salamanders, eggs, or fish, and will consume the young of other birds, reducing its popularity with bird lovers.

Migration Habits

Found year-round in the Midwest and East, these late migrants congregate by the thousands in late autumn and early spring. Attempts to control their huge flocks have been unsuccessful.

Placement of Feeders

Backyard feeders and public garbage bins alike are subject to raids by these aggressive scavengers. Cracked corn, mixed seeds, suet, and sunflower hearts are sure-fire lures.

Dickcissel

Once residing only in midwestern grasslands, this species established a new breeding population in New England in the nineteenth century, which mysteriously disappeared, but simultaneously expanded its range across the Midwest. These fluctuations continue, as local populations are unpredictable from year to year.

Description
From a visible perch, the vibrant bird issues an incessant hissing or buzzing *dick-dick-cissel* song. The 7-inch breeding male, streaked brown above with a yellow breast, black bib, and chestnut wing patch, is easy to spot.

Preferred Habitat
Croplands, hayfields, and pastures provide a ready supply of food and safe ground nesting sites for the polygamous dickcissel's two annual broods.

Feeding Habits
Seeds and grain gathered from crops are staples, but insects gleaned from grassy fields are a favorite as well.

Migration Habits
An impressive traveling range, most dickcissels fly south to winter in Venezuela and return annually. Traveling in large flocks like clouds of insects, they can be found in the summer from Texas north throughout the Midwest.

Placement of Feeders
Expect those who flock to your backyard feeders to be regulars. They will be faithful visitors to your home every season.

RANGE MAP

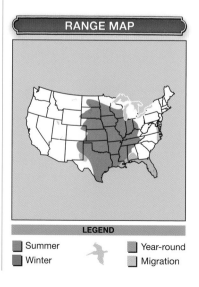

LEGEND

- Summer
- Winter
- Year-round
- Migration

Originally named "dunlings," meaning little dun-coloreds, these small, plump sandpipers measure only 6–8 inches.

Description

Breeding adults are reddish above and white below, with a large black patch on the belly. Winter adults are grayish brown above and whitish below. The best field mark is their long, black, downward-curving bill.

Preferred Habitat

The male reaches breeding grounds in Arctic or subalpine tundra in early June and awaits his devoted mate's arrival. Together they build a ground nest, sharing incubation and feeding the chicks. During migration and winter, dunlins can be found on mud flats, beaches along ponds, lakes, or oceans.

brown

Feeding Habits

This species consumes small marine animals, crustaceans, mollusks, and insect larvae. They particularly favor marine worms, which minimizes competition with other shorebirds.

Migration Habits

Usually seen along the Pacific, Gulf, and Atlantic Coasts, these birds breed across the northern states. Their migration takes them throughout the eastern half of the United States.

Placement of Feeders

In winter dunlins form large flocks of up to tens of thousands, but they do not mingle with other species. They are tame and can be approached quite easily.

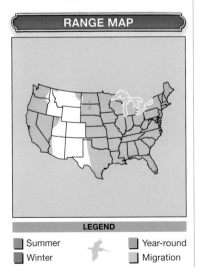

RANGE MAP

LEGEND

■ Summer   ■ Year-round
■ Winter   ■ Migration

Grasshopper Sparrow

Named for its insect-like song, a male grasshopper sparrow perches on a dried weed stalk singing *kip-kip-kip-zeee*, then flits off to chase a female, emitting sounds too high-pitched for human hearing. The clever female can make a display of injury to lure away predators, and conceals the location of the nest by walking to it through tall grass.

Description
This small grassland sparrow, measuring only 5 inches, is dark, scaly-patterned rust above, with a buff breast, pale stripe on crown, short pointed tail, and dark eyes.

Preferred Habitat
Grassland options vary by region, but the grasshopper sparrow prefers open, weedy meadows or pastures, including airports. Their populations tend to decline as overgrown fields are cleared for urban development.

Feeding Habits
Foraging among grass clumps, this bird eats seeds, spiders, grasshoppers, and other insects.

Migration Habits
The northern two-thirds of the United States (and, rarely, Florida) are breeding grounds for the bird, where they nest in loose colonies. When the weather turns, they winter across parts of the southern United States.

Placement of Feeders
If you have the option, mow or cultivate paddocks and hayfields late in summer to avoid destroying their ground-level nests.

RANGE MAP

LEGEND

■ Summer   ■ Year-round
■ Winter   ■ Migration

Gray-cheeked Thrush

In a scraggly tree, a male gray-cheek pipes its sweet, fluting song for up to 20 hours of daylight. This thrush could be missed, since they are fairly quiet during migration and are heard less commonly than the Swainson's or hermit thrushes.

Description
This 8-inch thrush is dull brown or olive-brown above and whitish below, with large dark spots on the breast and neck. The species is named for its gray cheek patch.

Preferred Habitat
In stark contrast to their South American rainforest wintering grounds, the birds breed in sub-Arctic woodlands and willow and alder thickets. Females construct a nest of mud and plants near or on the ground.

Feeding Habits
The ground-foraging thrush ingests mainly ants, but also spiders, earthworms, caterpillars, mollusks, beetles, and fruit.

Migration Habits
This bird's bi-annual journey of up to 8,000 miles is a greater distance than any other thrush travels. Like the Swainson's thrush, this nighttime migrant risks collisions with tall buildings and TV towers.

Placement of Feeders
In spring and autumn the gray-cheeked species is common and widespread, but easily overlooked as it spends most of its time quietly foraging on the ground.

RANGE MAP

LEGEND

- Summer
- Winter
- Year-round
- Migration

Green Heron

brown

Startled from the edge of a reedy pond, a compact, dark-colored bird utters a sharp *kowp* call and explodes into flight. This shy bird, formerly called the green-backed heron, avoids the open habitats of other herons and is less commonly sighted.

Description
Significantly smaller than other herons at 16–22 inches, the green heron has a dark head, gray-green or gray-blue back, chestnut cheeks and neck, and bright orange or yellow legs.

Preferred Habitat
Nesting in isolated pairs or small colonies, green herons are drawn to freshwater or brackish marshes, rivers, ponds, or streams with muddy banks and thick clumps of weeds or trees for cover.

Feeding Habits
Crouching, log-like, on the muddy bank, the patient hunter dangles a leaf from its bill to attract fish to the surface. Stretching its neck, the heron takes aim, flicks its tail nervously, and stabs an unsuspecting fish. Frogs, crustaceans, and insects are also prey for the diminutive heron.

Migration Habits
The green heron is an annual summer resident of the Midwest. This species is widespread east of the Rockies and along coastal California, southern Arizona, and Texas.

Placement of Feeders
Approach carefully and quietly to spot the green heron hunting at the edge of a water source.

RANGE MAP

LEGEND

■ Summer	■ Year-round
■ Winter	■ Migration

A lovely, hymn-like fluting song at twilight has earned the hermit thrush much admiration. Its long, rolling notes vary in pitch and volume, making it difficult to pinpoint the songster.

Description
The 7.5-inch thrush is olive-brown above and boldly spotted buff below. The face is gray with a white eye ring, but the best field mark is its reddish tail.

Preferred Habitat
This forest bird can be found in coniferous or deciduous woodlands or wooded swamps, bogs, and fields. The female builds a well-concealed ground nest, and the male helpfully feeds his incubating mate.

Feeding Habits
In spring and summer the bird forages on the ground and gleans vegetation for ants, butterflies, bees, moths, and spiders. In winter they subsist on wild fruits, buds, and berries.

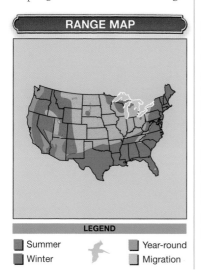

RANGE MAP

LEGEND

Summer
Winter
Year-round
Migration

Migration Habits
When you spot a spotted thrush in winter, it must be the hermit thrush. As soon as beetles emerge in early spring, they head north through the Midwest, into the Rocky Mountain range and along the Pacific Northwest Coast.

Placement of Feeders
Suet cakes, raw apples, pecans, and peanut butter may attract this woodland bird to a backyard feeder. Watch for its characteristic tail-bobbing; this is the only thrush to wag its tail.

Horned Lark

brown

Of the world's 75 true lark species, the horned lark is the only one widespread in North America. The clearing of eastern forests made way for this bird of open spaces, which often makes its home on prairies, air fields, farmland, or Arctic tundra.

Description

Although its black "horns" are rarely visible, the 8-inch lark is very distinct with its black markings on the head and black crescent band across the breast. The face is white or yellow and the black tail is rimmed with white.

Preferred Habitat

In a spectacular courtship display, males soar to heights of up to 800 feet, then nose-dive silently back down. Their nests—in a shallow depression on the bare ground—are vulnerable to late storms or spring planting.

Feeding Habits

Walking slowly along the ground and scratching with its large feet, the horned lark searches for grain, seeds, insects, or spiders.

Migration Habits

This bird breeds all across the United States except in the Southeast and is a year-round resident of the Midwest.

Placement of Feeders

Larks gather in flocks of up to thousands in late autumn, often joining with longspurs and buntings. They may be seen along roadsides or croplands, often singing in flight.

RANGE MAP

LEGEND

■ Summer   ■ Year-round

■ Winter   ■ Migration

In an effort to control crop pests, house sparrows were imported from England in 1850 and released all over the United States. They have since spread throughout the entire continent, where they thrive in human-altered environments (part of their Latin name is *domesticus*). Unfortunately, these aggressive competitors have diminished the success of native cavity nesters such as bluebirds and tree swallows.

Description
Males, up to 6.5 inches long, have a gray crown and rump, black bib, white cheeks, and chestnut head stripes, while the female and young are streaky brown above and white below.

Preferred Habitat
Resourceful and friendly, the house sparrow is at home in cities, suburbs,

and farmland, where it constructs nests of grass, feathers, and bits of rubbish in a manmade or natural cavity.

Feeding Habits
The sparrow squabbles fiercely over territory, mates, and food, the latter including insects, grains, berries, and weed seeds.

Migration Habits
Some birds of the past experienced involuntary migration, touring the country by rail while snacking on spilled grain in train cars, but the house sparrow has become an abundant permanent resident throughout North America.

Placement of Feeders
A familiar sight at every backyard feeder, house sparrows are drawn to bread crumbs, seeds, and grain.

brown

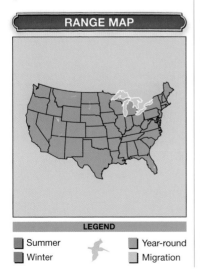

RANGE MAP

LEGEND

Summer

Winter

Year-round

Migration

it nests in a shallow depression in the ground.

Feeding Habits

Like other plovers, killdeers feed with a stop-start action of chasing prey and standing still, then pecking in the dirt with their bills to seek seeds and insects, earthworms, and snails.

Migration Habits

As early as February, some killdeers migrate north to breed. However, they can be found throughout the Midwest every summer.

Placement of Feeders

Killdeers are common and easy to identify, but if you spot an adult male giving the broken-wing display, retreat and do not disturb him.

brown

Nearly every vacant lot or golf course is home to this noisy plover. When threatened, the adult bird feigns injury, dragging its wing as if broken, to lure predators away from the nest. These shorebirds flee by sprinting along the ground or swimming to safety.

Description

Named for its shrill *kill-deer* alarm call, the species measures 9–11 inches, colored brown above and white below, with a rust-colored rump, long legs, and a black-and-white tipped tail. Adults have two identifying black bands across the chest, though chicks have only one.

Preferred Habitat

Any short-grassed open field, river bank, or gravel road edge with water nearby can house the killdeer, where

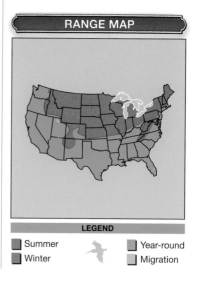

RANGE MAP

LEGEND

Summer — Year-round

Winter — Migration

The polygamous male builds up to 20 "dummy" nests to serve as courting sites for potential mates. Interested females then construct their own nests. This abundance of nests, most unused, makes it difficult for competing species to enact revenge when the marsh wren pierces the eggs of nearby wrens and larger blackbirds.

brown

Description

Smaller than a sparrow at 4–5.5 inches, the wren is brown above, pale buff below, with a white-streaked back and white eyebrow. Males define and defend their territory with up to 200 different songs.

Preferred Habitat

The marsh wren prefers wetlands, particularly freshwater or brackish marshes with abundant cattails, bullrushes, or reeds. These plants are used to construct a nest attached to reeds.

Feeding Habits

This flycatcher consumes aphids, beetles, wasps, bees, mites, and larval dragonflies, and plucks other aquatic insects and snails from their marshy home.

Migration Habits

This bird has an extensive breeding range spanning the United States from north to south. It can be found each summer throughout the Midwest.

Placement of Feeders

Patient observation in the bird's habitat may be rewarded with a brief glimpse of its cocked tail. Listen for the male's call, reminiscent of a mechanical sewing machine.

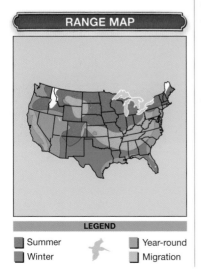

RANGE MAP

LEGEND

Summer
Winter
Year-round
Migration

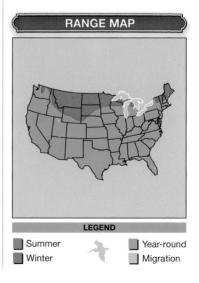

Feeding Habits

Like other doves and pigeons, this dove feeds its young regurgitated, protein-rich food known as "pigeon milk" produced in the adult's gullet. Birds may fly several miles at dawn or dusk in search of seeds, insects, or the nearest water source.

Migration Habits

Hundreds of birds may congregate for autumn migration from the Pacific Northwest south throughout the continental United States.

Placement of Feeders

The backyard birder has only to listen for the dove's song to recognize this frequent feeder visitor. Watch for their fast, smooth silhouettes flying at early morning or dusk.

brown

With 70 million shot annually, the mourning dove ranks as America's most popular game bird. The species boomed with the large-scale felling of forests, and its mournful *coo-ah, coo, coo* song is recognizable in all urban and suburban environments.

Description

This 12-inch sandy-colored dove has black wing spots and a long tapered tail bordered with white. Males are slightly brighter, with a pink sheen along the neck.

Preferred Habitat

The resilient mourning dove thrives from farmland to irrigated deserts, open fields, parks, and lawns. You will find their stick nests in tall trees, low bushes, or on the ground.

RANGE MAP

LEGEND

■ Summer   ■ Year-round

■ Winter   ■ Migration

A loud, repeated *flicker* or *wick-wick-wick* ringing in the forest canopy announces the breeding season of this unusual woodpecker. Three color variations exist—yellow-shafted (East), red-shafted (West), and gilded (Southwest)—but they interbreed where their ranges overlap.

Description

Large at 10–14 inches, flickers are black or brown with tan bars above, with a pale spotted breast and bright underwings. Eastern birds have yellow under the wings, a red nape, and a black "mustache" on males. Western birds have red underwings, rump, and mustache.

Preferred Habitat

Spot the flicker in open country near large trees, such as farmlands, parks, woodlands, deserts, and suburbs. They

brown

nest in a tree cavity or burrow into fence posts, rafters, or even saguaro cacti.

Feeding Habits

Foraging on the ground, the flicker extends its enormous tongue to lap up ants. It also consumes insects, fruit, and seeds, occasionally flycatching.

Migration Habits

Although year-round residents of the United States, these birds migrate north for the breeding season and return south to winter in Texas and in the Desert Southwest.

Placement of Feeders

Watch for these ground feeders eating ants and beetles on lawns or sidewalks. They may also visit suet feeders.

RANGE MAP

LEGEND
- Summer
- Winter
- Year-round
- Migration

brown

N uthatches have an inexplicable habit of spreading layers of pine resin around the outside of the nesting cavity while they raise their young. The pitch sometimes smears on the adults' feathers, making them look messy.

Description

This small, stocky bird, only 5 inches long, is blue-gray above with a black crown (gray on females) and rusty red below. They are the only nuthatches with a white eyebrow and a black stripe through the eye.

Preferred Habitat

A preference for conifers makes these birds more numerous in the North and the West, but they expand their range during winter. Like all nuthatches, these birds nest in cavities, usually raising their young in a dead tree.

Feeding Habits

Clinging with long toes, the nuthatch creeps up and down tree trunks, foraging in pine cones for conifer seeds and insects, and using its strong beak to crack open seeds.

Migration Habits

Sparse food supplies send these birds south. They breed across northern states but can be found year-round throughout New England the Upper Midwest and western United States.

Placement of Feeders

Though less common than its white-breasted relative, the red-breast will visit seed or suet feeders and use a birdhouse. Its nasally *yank-yank* call is higher pitched than the white-breast.

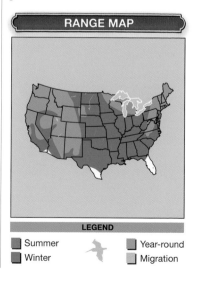

RANGE MAP

LEGEND

Summer — Year-round

Winter — Migration

Continuous singing from the forest canopy allows birders to readily identify this vireo, the most abundant bird in eastern deciduous forests.

Description

This small songbird, measuring 5 inches, is olive-brown above and whitish below. From the crown, identifying marks include its blue-gray cap, white eyebrow, and red iris.

Preferred Habitat

Vireos are common in deciduous and mixed forest, as well as urban and residential areas with mature trees. Females lay eggs in an open cup of twigs and bark suspended in forked branches. Unfortunately, this species is the most common victim of the brown-headed cowbird's nest parasitism.

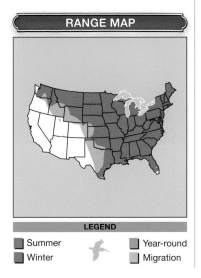

RANGE MAP

LEGEND

- Summer
- Winter
- Year-round
- Migration

brown

Feeding Habits

Scooting along a branch, the vireo plucks a fat caterpillar with its foot, lifting it to its mouth one bite at a time. Insects comprise nearly 90 percent of its summer diet, but in winter most birds subsist on fruit.

Migration Habits

Singly and in pairs, vireos make an annual migration to their breeding range east of the Rockies and north into the Pacific Northwest.

Placement of Feeders

Watch for this persistent vocalist perched high in the treetops. The vireo's presence may be revealed by its song, a series of slurred phrases—*Here I am! See me, see me?*—separated by short pauses.

Seventeen races of this species are recognized, varying in color and weight. These regional variations develop because most savannah sparrows return year after year to the area where they hatched.

Description
Plumages vary from pale brown to darker chestnut above and pale below. Most races, measuring 4–6 inches, have a pale stripe through the crown.

Preferred Habitat
The aptly named sparrow is found in large open spaces of short grass and weeds, from tundra to marshland to golf courses. Beneath a shrub or tuft of grass the female weaves a shallow nest of grass, often home to two broods each season. Males maintain several mates.

Feeding Habits
This sparrow is a ground dweller, running and hopping in search of grasshoppers, ants, and spiders. Insects make up most of the sparrow's diet in summer, while in winter they frequently roost among sorghum crops, a source of seeds through the cold months.

Migration Habits
Breeding grounds for this bird span the Pacific Northwest and into the Midwest. It winters across the southern third of the United States from the East to West Coasts.

Placement of Feeders
Identify this sparrow in your backyard by noting the bird's darkly streaked underparts, its short, notched tail, and the yellow spots in front of the eyes.

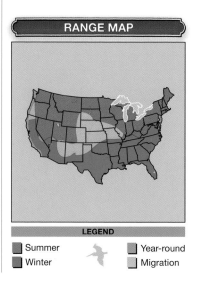

RANGE MAP

LEGEND

Summer   Year-round

Winter   Migration

The stunning scissor-tail is a noisy and aggressive bird, impossible to ignore. The long tail for which they are named allows an impressive acrobatic aerial display during spring courtship that frequently includes backward somersaults.

Description
A long, forked dark tail makes up more than half of the bird's 14 inches. Adults are pale whitish above, with bright pink on their sides and belly. Juveniles have a shorter tail and lack the pink markings.

Preferred Habitat
These large, solitary birds prefer open country, roadsides, and ranches, where they build a bulky stick nest in an isolated tree. Larger birds and predators are readily attacked by the aggressive parents.

brown

Feeding Habits
Feeding on the ground, in trees, or on the wing like other flycatchers, this species consumes many insects, especially grasshoppers, beetles, and crickets, as well as agricultural pests.

Migration Habits
Its range may be expanding northeastward, but it generally breeds in Texas and neighboring states, with a smaller population in southern Florida, usually wintering in Central and South America.

Placement of Feeders
For most birders the scissor-tail ranks as a must-see. In southern Texas they are a common sight perched on fence posts and wires along roads, giving a harsh *kee-kee-kee-kee* call.

RANGE MAP

LEGEND

Summer		Year-round
Winter		Migration

Song Sparrow

brown

From spring breeding season through autumn, and even into winter in the North, the aptly named song sparrow serenades his mate with more than 20 different songs, improvising more than 1,000 variations on these melodies.

Description

Coloring varies from rust to gray to streaked brown above, but all measure 5–7 inches long, with a brown eyebrow and a central spot in a streaked white breast. Juveniles lack the central breast spot and may be mistaken for the savannah sparrow.

Preferred Habitat

Song sparrows make their homes in thickets, gardens, parks, and roadsides, where they raise up to three broods each year. Fledglings begin to develop their own song repertoire before they even leave the nest.

Feeding Habits

These ground feeders use their feet to rustle up insects, seeds, grain, and berries. In flight, watch the sparrow's characteristic pumping of its long, rounded tail.

Migration Habits

Traveling solo or in pairs, song sparrows are found throughout the United States year-round, but winter from the Deep South into the Desert Southwest.

Placement of Feeders

Although common and widespread in North America, a song sparrow at a backyard feeder is a rare occasion. But if you locate a nearby nesting pair, watch for them to return year after year.

RANGE MAP

LEGEND

■ Summer	■ Year-round
■ Winter	■ Migration

Once known as the bay-winged bunting, this familiar farmland sparrow was renamed for its sweet serenade to the setting sun. This ground dweller alights on the highest available perch to sing its descending trill throughout the day, but it is the only sparrow to sing regularly at twilight.

Description

The 6.5-inch vesper sparrow is streaked gray-brown above and pale and streaked below. Its white-rimmed tail and orange-red shoulder patches are the best identifying field marks.

Preferred Habitat

This bird is one of only a handful of species common in prairies, fields, meadows, and roadsides in farm country. The nest is sunk into a shallow dent in the ground, leaving their broods vulnerable to the

threat of early mowing or cultivation.

Feeding Habits

Running along the ground, the vesper sparrow halts to pick up grain, weed seeds, and insects. Its fondness for agricultural pests, such as weevils make it a welcome addition to cultivated fields.

Migration Habits

The coastal states, from California to New England, are wintering grounds for these songsters, but summers are spent in the Midwest and the northern United States.

Placement of Feeders

Scatter cracked corn below your feeding stations to draw solo birds or mating pairs in winter and early spring.

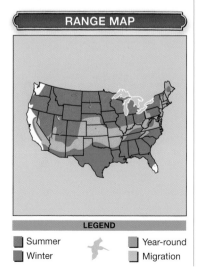

RANGE MAP

LEGEND

- Summer
- Winter
- Year-round
- Migration

brown

A loud, deep song echoes in the summer night. *Whip-poor-will, whip-poor-will* thrums over and over, announcing that the elusive, nocturnal whip-poor-will is perched somewhere nearby.

Description

The 10-inch bird's coloring—mottled brown above with a black throat—provides excellent camouflage among the leaf litter on the forest floor. Males have white tips on their outer tail feathers that are visible in flight, but the female has an all-brown tail.

Preferred Habitat

By day the whip-poor-will sleeps on the forest floor in dry open woodlands near fields. Eggs are laid among dead leaves, and within days of hatching, the young seek a secure hiding place, where their parents feed them regurgitated insects until they can fly.

Feeding Habits

Nighttime insects comprise the whip-poor-will's diet, especially moths caught on the wing. The bird can even swallow a grasshopper whole.

Migration Habits

There is a smaller population in New Mexico and western Texas, but the primary population breeds from the north-central states south to Kansas and east to the coast, wintering from the Gulf Coast southward.

Placement of Feeders

Birders are more likely to hear than to see these birds, but you may catch a glimpse of their eyes reflecting red in car headlights.

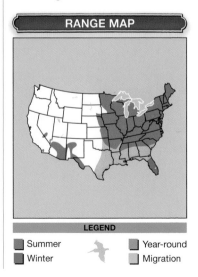

RANGE MAP

LEGEND

- Summer
- Winter
- Year-round
- Migration

P raised by American author Henry David Thoreau as the most beautiful song of any bird, the male wood thrush sings his sweet, liquid melody *ee-o-lay, ee-o-lay* at dawn and again at dusk, sometimes joined by the female's equally lovely song from the nest.

Description
At up to 8.5 inches, the starling-sized wood thrush is the largest bird of its family in the East. Adults are olive-brown above and dark-spotted white below. The bird's face is streaked black and white, and its crown is reddish.

Preferred Habitat
In damp mature forests, parks, and gardens with large shade trees, the mating pair combines mud, grasses, and moss to craft a sturdy nest for the season's two broods. Nests are frequently parasitized by brown-headed cowbirds.

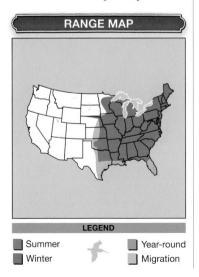

RANGE MAP

LEGEND

■ Summer   ■ Year-round
■ Winter   ■ Migration

Feeding Habits
The thrush's springtime diet consists almost entirely of insects, such as beetles, ants, and butterflies, but by late summer it eats mainly plants, berries, and seeds.

Migration Habits
In late April flocks migrate to the Midwest and east to the Atlantic.

Placement of Feeders
This is the only thrush to regularly nest near human dwellings, but they seldom visit feeding stations. They are welcome residents in gardens, because they eat cutworms and beetles.

brown

Feeding Habits

In spring, when insects are plentiful, they account for up to 50% of the goldfinch's diet. Seeds are its main staple through late summer and autumn, with berries supplementing in winter.

Migration Habits

Spring is ideal breeding time in western states, but in the East, goldfinches commonly wait until late summer, when weed seeds are readily available. They travel in flocks of up to 20, but are hardy enough to winter across much of their normal range.

Placement of Feeders

Feeders offering nigel thistle seeds and sunflower seeds are sure to draw these birds to your yard, and they are frequent visitors during the winter months. The goldfinch also loves birdbaths.

This finch is commonly known as the wild canary for its appearance and song. As it hops along summer fields gleaning thistle seeds, the male bird's bright yellow and black plumage is unmistakable.

Description

The summer breeding male is easily recognized, with its lemon-yellow coloring, and black cap, wings, and tail. At 5 inches long, the female and winter male are significantly duller yellow with black wings and tail.

Preferred Habitat

Fields, groves, thickets, farmland, and weedy grasslands provide a steady supply of small insects and seeds year-round.

yellow

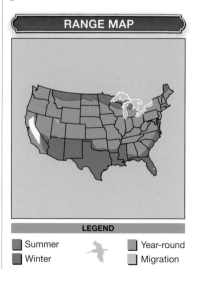

RANGE MAP

LEGEND

Summer   Year-round
Winter   Migration

U ntil 1997, this bird was classified as a solitary vireo, but is now distinguished as a distinct species. The attractively colored blue-headed vireo is a fairly common migrant, seen earlier in the spring than other vireos. It is extremely tame and not threatened by human presence.

Description
Olive green above and white below, with yellowish flanks, the 6-inch, sparrow-sized vireo features a slate blue head with bold white spectacle markings.

Preferred Habitat
The blue-headed species is the only vireo to inhabit coniferous forests, where it nests in the forked twigs of small trees.

Feeding Habits
Like other vireos (and distinct from wrens), these slow fliers scan the trees for insects, hovering to pluck caterpillars, wasps, moths, butterflies, stink bugs, beetles, ants, spiders, or bees. Berries of dogwood trees may also catch this deliberate feeder's interest.

Migration Habits
Unique among vireos for their solo migrations, these birds are found in the eastern half of the United States, wintering in South Carolina and southward along the Gulf Coast.

Placement of Feeders
Friendly and fearless, these curious birds are comfortable on human territory. Listen for their slow, slurred calls. They have even been known to sit quietly and allow their feathers to be stroked.

RANGE MAP

LEGEND

Summer

Winter

Year-round

Migration

yellow

Feeding Habits
Hovering low over a clump of cattails, the yellowthroat scoops up adult and larval insects such as spiders or dragonflies, supplementing its diet with seeds.

Migration Habits
Migrating from South and Central America into the entire United States during summer, this species is the northernmost yellowthroat in the western hemisphere. Though not its usual habitat, the migrating birds may be found far from water.

Placement of Feeders
This shy but curious species can be roused from their tall-grass hideouts by various noises. Try making a squeaking noise by kissing the back of your thumb, give a low growl, or make a *psssh-psssh* sound.

O ften called the Maryland yellow-throat, where it was first collected in 1766, this sweet songbird is elusive and rarely seen. The male yellow-throat twitters from perch to perch, marking his territory and defending it aggressively.

yellow

Description
The small black-masked male issues a sharp *chek* call from his bright yellow throat. The 6-inch female, lacking the mask, responds with a gentle *wichity, wichity* song.

Preferred Habitat
Brushy swamps, wet thickets, or over-grown marshes, and tangles of weeds or berry bushes provide sufficient cover for the ground nests of these polyga-mous birds.

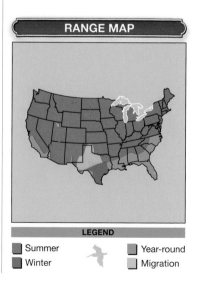

RANGE MAP

LEGEND
Summer   Year-round
Winter   Migration

Although actually in the blackbird family, the meadowlark is so named for its singing ability. The eastern and western meadowlarks are identical in appearance, habitat, and feeding and nesting habits, but have vastly different songs. A clear, high-pitched, wistful trill of *see seer seee-u* sets the eastern meadowlark apart from its western counterpart's longer, confident, gurgling song.

Description

Streaked black and brown on top and measuring 8–10.5 inches, this species has an eye-catching lemon yellow and black breast. The western species is paler and grayer.

Preferred Habitat

Weaving blades of prairie grass to make a dome, the female meadowlark constructs her ground nests in grasslands, pastures, and marshes. If the nest is destroyed by mowing, these polygamous breeders will nest again.

Feeding Habits

Grain and seeds round out a diet comprised mostly of insects, including spiders, beetles, grasshoppers, crickets, caterpillars, weevils, ants, and wasps.

Migration Habits

Traveling in groups bright meadowlarks can be found in almost any grassy, open area. They occupy the eastern United States year-round, migrating slightly northward in summer.

Placement of Feeders

Look for these shy feeders perched on fence posts. They may be drawn to seeds and grain spread on the ground.

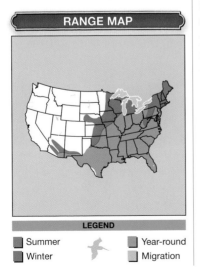

RANGE MAP

LEGEND

■ Summer
■ Winter
■ Year-round
■ Migration

yellow

Evening Grosbeak

Birders unfamiliar with this species might describe it as a huge American goldfinch. But note the large, powerful beaks for which they are named.

Description

Grosbeaks are stout and round with short tails. Males are olive brown above and yellowish below, while females are grayish above. Males are easily identified by the dark head, bright yellow forehead band, and white wing patches.

Preferred Habitat

Generally this bird lives in spruce and conifer forests, only venturing into residential areas for sunflower seeds. High in a conifer the female builds a loose, fragile nest of twigs and moss.

Feeding Habits

In summer this species consumes large quantities of insects, but their conical bills are also well suited to cracking seeds and buds.

Migration Habits

The introduction of box elder and maple trees, as well as feeding stations, has drawn these birds eastward to the Atlantic. However, they can still be found year-round throughout the the Pacific Northwest, the Upper Midwest and Upper New England.

Placement of Feeders

Flocks of friendly, social evening grosbeaks are easily lured to a backyard feeding station featuring sunflower seeds, where they may remain for a few hours or a few months. Their ringing *cleer* call sounds like a loud house sparrow.

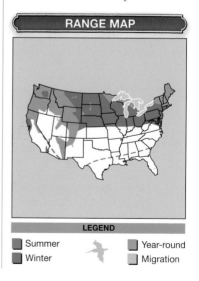

RANGE MAP

LEGEND

Summer · Year-round
Winter · Migration

This bird is closely related to the blue-winged warbler, and these species interbreed where their ranges overlap, producing fertile hybrid offspring called Brewster's warblers; these offspring, in turn, produce Lawrence's warblers. The hybrid birds have coloring similar to either parent species, but with yellower bellies.

Description

Resembling a chickadee, the 4.5 inch male is gray above, white below, with a black mask and throat, yellow crown and wing patch, and white spots underneath the tail. The female has a gray mask and throat.

Preferred Habitat

Generally preferring drier areas than the blue-winged warbler, this ground-nesting species resides in overgrown fields and briar-rich pastures, abandoning fields when they become heavily forested.

Feeding Habits

The acrobatic warbler swings upside down to pick caterpillars and insects from the underside of foliage or hovers to snatch insects from leaves.

Migration Habits

Arriving in May, the warbler's short breeding season begins. By July, the fledglings leave the nest and the flocks return to South to warmer climates for the winter.

Placement of Feeders

If caterpillars are plentiful in your area, watch this colorful warbler consume mass quantities during migration.

yellow

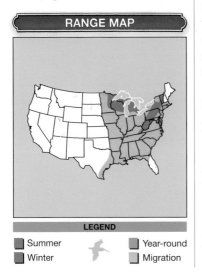

RANGE MAP

LEGEND

Summer

Winter

Year-round

Migration

yellow

In an overgrown field, a startled brown sparrow flaps jerkily just above the grass, then dives back to the ground to flee on foot. This elusive sparrow, named for nineteenth-century naturalist John Le Conte, only risks emerging to a perch to share its insect-like song.

Description

Overall yellow-brown coloring makes this sparrow easy to identify. Adults measure 5 inches, with a white crown stripe, wide streaked red collar, gray patch above the ear, and a pointed tail. Nonbreeding birds are yellowish and duller.

Preferred Habitat

For breeding, Le Conte's sparrow favors grassland and meadows bordering marshland, especially fields containing foxtail, where it nests in a grass clump on the ground. Dry, brushy fields are its home in winter.

Feeding Habits

A weak flyer, the bird scans the ground and low vegetation for seeds and insects, including grasshoppers, leafhoppers, and spiders.

Migration Habits

In the last century, this sparrow's breeding range has shifted north. It summers throughout the Upper Midwest.

Placement of Feeders

These stout sparrows are most numerous during their fall migration, though they rarely sing in this season. Unlike other sparrows, they can be approached quite closely when perched.

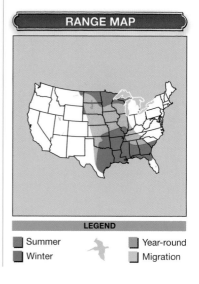

RANGE MAP

LEGEND

■ Summer   ■ Year-round
■ Winter   ■ Migration

In the chilly autumn air, a flock of small, dark-colored birds undulates through the sky, alternately bunching up and fanning out. The distinctive, rising *bzzzzt* song confirms the presence of pine siskins.

Description

This 5-inch finch has a dark, streaked back, a notched tail, and small patches of yellow on the wings and tail. In flight it looks like a sparrow, but the splashes of yellow are good field markers.

Preferred Habitat

Small groups of pine siskins build their nests in conifers just a few feet apart. Here they raise two broods, then travel to mixed woodlands, alder thickets, or overgrown pastures in search of winter food.

RANGE MAP

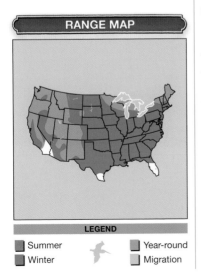

LEGEND

■ Summer ■ Year-round
■ Winter ■ Migration

Feeding Habits

Harvesting seeds of hemlocks, alders, birches, and cedars is the siskin's primary objective, but insects make up a small part of its diet as well.

Migration Habits

Though found throughout the West year-round, the siskin spends its winters in the Midwest and further east across the United States.

Placement of Feeders

Pine siskins, like other northern finches, are fond of salt and may be found along salted highways in winter. Thistle seeds are their feeder favorite, but backyard elm and ash trees can do the trick as well. Keeping your feeders full will ensure your chances of spotting this seasonal visitor.

yellow

cowbird, the warbler layers nest material over the unwelcome egg.

Feeding Habits

Like other warblers this species is entirely insectivorous. Males tend to search for food higher in the tree canopy than do the less conspicuous females.

Migration Habits

Warbler flocks arrive in late April in the northern two-thirds of the United States. They will be a bright addition to summer birdwatching. After a very short breeding season, the birds return to Mexico, and Central and South America for winter.

Placement of Feeders

As flocks migrate south in late July, listen for their sweet, clear seven-note song. Keep a watch out for this mid-summer visitor to your backyard.

A flash of bright yellow flitting into a backyard ornamental shrub may announce the presence of this 5-inch warbler, the only North American warbler to appear all yellow.

Description

Adult males are yellow-green above and bright yellow below, with two yellow tail patches and reddish stripes on the breast and belly. Juveniles and females are duller yellow to olive-green.

Preferred Habitat

A freshwater source and small trees are the ideal environment for yellow warbler colonies, commonly found in willow thickets, marshes, swamps, parks, and backyard gardens. Mating pairs construct strong nests in smalltrees. If parasitized by the brown-headed

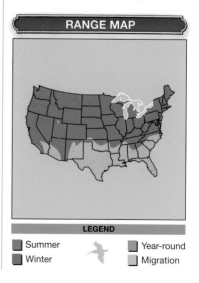

RANGE MAP

LEGEND

■ Summer ■ Year-round
■ Winter ■ Migration

This usually silent bird has a tendency to sing at the approach of a storm, earning it the nickname "rain crow." Its unique call is a rapid, rattling *ka-ka-ka-kow-kowp-kowp-kowp*.

Description

Slender and long-tailed, the bird measures 10–12.5 inches, colored brown above and white below, with a yellow and black bill. In flight, note the large white spots under the tail and the red patches on the wings.

Preferred Habitat

The cuckoo crafts a flimsy twig nest in a bush or a small sapling in orchards, damp thickets, overgrown fields, or suburban parks. Although not classified as a nest parasite, the cuckoo will sometimes lay eggs in its black-billed relative's nest or those of other birds.

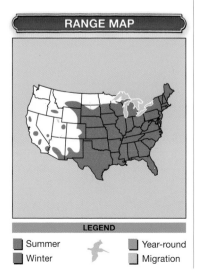

RANGE MAP

LEGEND

- ■ Summer
- ■ Winter
- ■ Year-round
- ■ Migration

Feeding Habits

A taste for hairy caterpillars and tent worms makes this bird useful for keeping agricultural pests in check. Their varied diet also includes fruit and berries, small bird eggs, and tiny amphibians.

Migration Habits

In spring the cuckoos travel north to the Central Plains and Midwest, then north to Minnesota and east to the coast.

Placement of Feeders

Even backyard cuckoo residents are shy and easily overlooked, as they rarely draw attention to themselves. Watch for them in late summer during temporary swarms of cicadas.

yellow

Feeding Habits

One of the few birds to cache food, the jay buries seeds and acorns for winter, indirectly planting new trees. Nuts, seeds, fruits, insects, mice, and bird fledglings comprise its diet.

Migration Habits

Traveling in flocks, these birds can be found from the eastern slopes of the Great Rockies to the Atlantic Coast. Its counterpart west of the Rockies is Steller's Jay.

Placement of Feeders

These backyard bullies are frequent feeder visitors in winter, and they love sunflower seeds, suet, cracked corn, and peanuts. They are comfortable around humans, but may mob birds, squirrels, cats, or even great horned owls.

These brightly colored, noisy birds have a mixed reputation. Both tame and curious, they warn other birds of danger and mob predators. Yet they also eat fledglings of other species and can imitate a hawk's screech or other bird calls to claim feeders for themselves.

blue

Description

At 12.5 inches, this large bird has an unmistakable bright blue crest, back, wings, and tail, with white tail tips, face, and underparts. Issuing a repertoire of boisterous calls, its own soft *queedle-queedle* song is seldom heard.

Preferred Habitat

Jays inhabit forests of all kinds, but oak forests are preferred. They are also common residents of gardens and parks.

RANGE MAP

LEGEND

Summer   Year-round

Winter   Migration

The incessantly active gnatcatcher cocks and flicks its long tail as it bounds through the branches. These tiny birds are fearless, readily attacking crows, jays, or other large predators who threaten their territory.

Description

Measuring 4–5.5 inches, the gnatcatcher is blue-gray above and white below with a long, black tail edged with white. Breeding males have an identifying black eyebrow, but in winter their gray eyebrow matches that of the female.

Preferred Habitat

In summer the bird is at home in open mixed woodlands, especially juniper groves. Its tiny lichen-decorated nest hooked to thin twigs is often parasitized by brown-headed cowbirds. As mating pairs take turns incubating the

eggs or feeding the fledglings, the male warbles incessantly at top volume.

Feeding Habits

This quick flyer can pursue fleeing insects through the treetops, hover to pick insects and spiders from leaves or flowers, or snatch tiny gnats from the air. In autumn they join mixed foraging flocks.

Migration Habits

Breeding throughout most of the United States gnatcatchers summer in several regions, one being the central Midwest.

Placement of Feeders

Track down this hyperactive bird by following its nasal *meehr* or buzzy *spee* call. Their high-pitched song will lead you right to their nest, which they don't attempt to conceal.

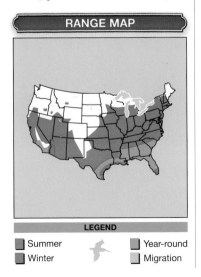

RANGE MAP

LEGEND

■ Summer ■ Year-round
■ Winter ■ Migration

blue

The habitat of choice for this warbler. Females construct nests on long branches of box elder trees, where their coloring provides good camouflage.

Feeding Habits

In the highest levels of the forest, these shy birds rummage in foliage for insects such as caterpillars.

Migration Habits

Unlike most birds, the cerulean warbler has a discontinuous range, breeding in loose colonies across the Northeast and Midwest and wintering in the tropics.

Placement of Feeders

The cerulean species is difficult to distinguish from other warblers, but with careful observation it can be sighted singing in treetops from dawn to dusk.

Although notoriously tough for bird-watchers to identify with any certainty because they live high in the forest canopy, try listening for series of quick, accelerating buzzing sounds and a higher buzzing drone to indicate the presence of these warblers. They may soon be added to the threatened species list as populations have reduced drastically in much of their range.

Description

Aptly named for its coloring, the 5-inch adult male is light blue above and white below, with a dark breast band. The female and juvenile look similar but are often tinged with green, lacking streaks or the breast band.

Preferred Habitat

Rich deciduous and mixed forests are

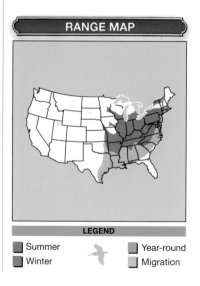

RANGE MAP

LEGEND

☐ Summer   ☐ Year-round
☐ Winter   ☐ Migration

During spring migration, from late March to early May, the colorful male finch, giving sharp *chip* calls in flight, is a common and welcome sight.

Description

Though similar to house finches and Cassin's finches, purple finches have a bluish-purple hue. Males, 5.5–6.5 inches long, are bluish-purple above and below, fading to a pale stomach. The sparrow-like female is brown, heavily streaked below, with whitish markings on her face.

Preferred Habitat

These finches usually nest in conifers, but that may include ornamental conifers in gardens or parks. They are also found in mixed and coniferous woodlands and bottomland forests.

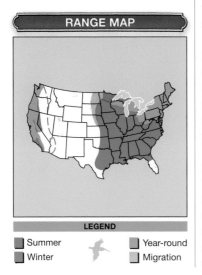

RANGE MAP

LEGEND

Summer
Winter
Year-round
Migration

Feeding Habits

Finches thrive on box elder, ash, and sycamore seeds, as well as maple, birch, and aspen buds. Fruit and berries provide sustenance in winter, and insects are a treat in summer.

Migration Habits

Generally these birds breed across most of Canada, but can also be found year-round along the Pacific Coast. But when food in the northern forests is scarce, purple finches flood their southern range.

Placement of Feeders

Year after year, small groups of purple finches return to their favorite feeders, especially those featuring sunflower seeds, where these birds lend a splash of color and a rich, cheery song to the winter landscape.

blue

are declining from competition with house sparrows and starlings.

Feeding Habits

Feeding on the wing, martins consume vast quantities of flying insects, especially dragonflies and airborne spiders.

Migration Habits

In late summer thousands of martins roost together in city shade trees, preparing for their migration south. They reach Canada in May, breeding along the Pacific states and the eastern half of the United States.

Placement of Feeders

Martin houses allow an up-close opportunity to observe these colorful birds, but in the West they can also be spotted at ponds or lakes, skimming the water to drink and bathe.

S outhern Native American tribes hung hollow gourds to encourage these useful insectivores to nest nearby, and the tradition continues in the East, where elaborate "hotel" dwellings are constructed to house entire martin colonies. Their pleasing song is a low-pitched rolling twitter.

Description

Recognizable as America's only all-dark swallow, the 7–8 inch bird has pointed wings and a forked tail. Males are glossy purple-black, while females are duller with gray underparts.

Preferred Habitat

Martins make their home in farmland, towns, marshes, deserts, or residential areas. Their populations

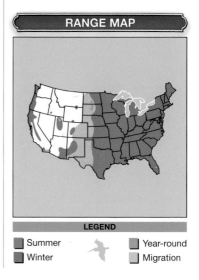

RANGE MAP

LEGEND
Summer
Winter
Year-round
Migration

A n Old English word for tail is "start" and the male's bright, reddish tail, which he constantly flashes and fans, earns the name. In their Latin American wintering grounds, redstarts are known as *candelita*, or "little flame."

Description
Adult males, at about 5 inches, are glossy black with flame-colored patches on the tail, wings, and sides year-round. Females and young males are pale olive to dark gray above with bright yellow highlights and a white belly.

Preferred Habitat
Redstarts make their home in mixed and deciduous second-growth forests along swamps or streams. The season's brood is raised in a tree-bound nest of moss and grass.

Feeding Habits
Restless and active, these small birds are always in motion, scanning foliage for tiny berries, dropping to the ground to munch on seeds, then zooming away to chase an insect with the aid of bristly feathers around the beak.

Migration Habits
Summering in the Upper Midwest, the breeding ground for the American redstart consists of most of the continental United States.

Placement of Feeders
Watch for a flash of black and orange in the treetops to find these common warblers, who usually respond with interest to birders making a "pishing" or squeaking sound.

RANGE MAP

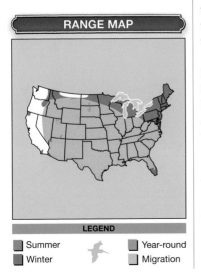

LEGEND

- ■ Summer
- ■ Winter
- ■ Year-round
- ■ Migration

black

This and the western Bullock's oriole are sometimes classified as the same species, the northern oriole. With the planting of trees across the Great Plains, their ranges overlapped and these distinct-looking birds began to interbreed.

Description

Males are unmistakable, with their black back and head, bright orange belly, black wings barred with white, and orange in the wings and tail. Females have a hint of orange. Juveniles look like females, and the juveniles of both races are nearly identical.

Preferred Habitat

In May the oriole constructs a pendulous pouch nest in the fork of a shade tree to raise its annual brood. In winter look for their beautifully woven nests in bare branches as evidence of their summer residences.

Feeding Habits

Seated in the forest canopy the oriole collects caterpillars, insects, and mulberries, then swoops to ground level to drain nectar from flowers.

Migration Habits

These orioles breed in the East and the Midwest, with the Bullock's covering the West and into Canada. In early September, they migrate south to winter in Mexico and South America.

Placement of Feeders

Before you sight them you will likely hear their clear, whistled *tea-dear-dear-dear* song. The best backyard draws are orange halves, grape jelly, suet, and nectar feeders.

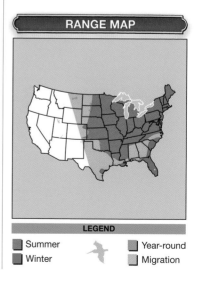

RANGE MAP

LEGEND

- Summer
- Winter
- Year-round
- Migration

black

Long ago abandoning natural nesting sites for docks, bridges, and barns, this swallow is a common sight in rural and suburban communities. Its forked tail is easily recognizable in flight, and it's the only swallow that flaps continuously, issuing a constant stream of twittering and chattering.

Description

Measuring 5-7 inches long, with a deeply forked tail and pointed wings, the barn swallow is dark blue-black above, with a red throat and pale undersides. Its flight is fast and direct, and may skim close to the ground.

Preferred Habitat

This bird favors open country or marshes near buildings and water, such as golf courses, parks, and farms.

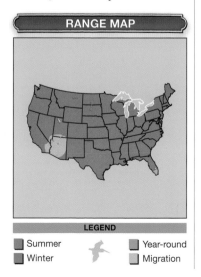

RANGE MAP

LEGEND

- Summer
- Winter
- Year-round
- Migration

It constructs nest made of mud pellets under building eaves or on a beam.

Feeding Habits

They capture insects on the wing, and thus spend more time in flight than almost any other bird. Like other swallows, they skim the surface of rivers or lakes to drink while flying.

Migration Habits

Wintering outside the United States presents no great challenge, as the swallow travels up to 600 miles or more to reach its summer breeding grounds throughout the lower 48 states of the U.S.

Placement of Feeders

Encourage the presence of these helpful insectivores by allowing them to nest in buildings or other man-made structures.

Black Tern

Destruction of its marsh habitat has led to drastically reduced populations of these elegant terns. Since its appearance on the Audubon Society's Blue List of threatened species in 1971, efforts continue to preserve and protect its wetland home.

Description
This large bird, measuring 9–10.5 inches, is unmistakable in all seasons. Breeding adults are all black, with a grayish tail and white highlights on the wings. Winter birds are gray above, with a black cap, and patchy white below with white side patches.

Preferred Habitat
Alongside freshwater marshes, lagoons, and lakes, black terns build a small hollow nest on floating marsh plants.

Social and gregarious, these terns usually nest and roost in colonies numbering a few to hundreds of birds.

Feeding Habits
This tern occasionally dives into freshwater for fish and crustaceans, but spends most of its time swooping erratically after flying insects.

Migration Habits
Their summer breeding range stretches from California to New England. In autumn they head south and seaward, wintering at sea or along the coasts of Central America, South America, or even far-flung Africa.

Placement of Feeders
Watch for this carnivore feeding along inland lakes and marshes. Listen for their nasal song or short *kik* call.

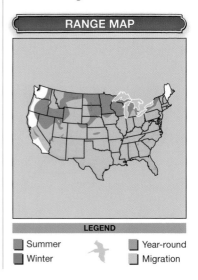

RANGE MAP

LEGEND

- Summer
- Winter
- Year-round
- Migration

black

Black-and-white Warbler

A thin, 5-inch bird striped black and white all over creeps down a tree trunk. Sometimes nicknamed the black-and-white creeper or nuthatch for its unusual tree-creeping habits, this unmistakable zebra-patterned bird is the oddball of the warbler family.

Description
The male has a black mask and throat in summer, but in winter the throat is white. Females have a white face and throat with a black stripe through the eye. Juveniles are patterned with brown instead of black.

Preferred Habitat
In deciduous and mixed forests of the North and East, these warblers can be found building grass nests concealed with dead leaves on or near the ground at the base of a tree, shrub, rock, or log.

Feeding Habits
Even before the spring leaves unfold, this warbler scours branches and tree trunks upside down, poking into loose bark for insects and larvae, especially spiders and daddy longlegs.

Migration Habits
As early as March flocks appear in the East, heading north to breed. By July the birds are ready to head south, wintering along parts of the Gulf Coast to South America.

Placement of Feeders
Track down their high-pitched, creaky-hinge song of six to eight *wee-see* phrases to observe this cooperative, friendly warbler.

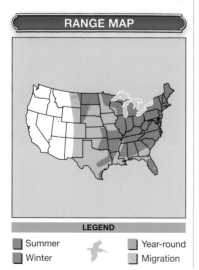

RANGE MAP

LEGEND

■ Summer   ■ Year-round
■ Winter   ■ Migration

black

Blackburnian Warbler

Scientists recently discovered that although this warbler is similar to four other warblers that may share a common food source and even perch in the same conifer, each species uses different foraging techniques and lives at a different level from the ground.

Description

The spring male is streaked with black and white, with a bright orange throat, eyebrow, and crown patch. The female is similar but more yellow and grayish, with two identifying brace marks on her back. The 5-inch creature issues thin, fast, high-pitched calls *sleet-sleet-sleet* and *tiddly-tiddly-tiddly*.

Preferred Habitat

Coniferous forests, as well as oak-hickory woodlands in southeastern mountain ranges, provide high perches for these foragers.

Feeding Habits

Like several other warblers, the Blackburnian warbler dines on insects and berries.

Migration Habits

Your best chance of spotting these otherwise elusive birds is from the last week of April through mid-May, as their migration takes them through the Midwest and the Northeast in large flocks.

Placement of Feeders

These shy critters are best identified by their call and then sought among the high treetops, where they may appear at the ends of branches searching for bugs among the foliage.

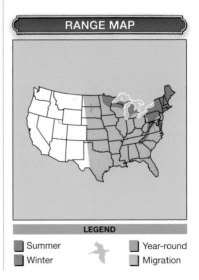

RANGE MAP

LEGEND

■ Summer ■ Year-round
■ Winter ■ Migration

black

In gardens and forests across North America the chickadee's acrobatic antics and sweet *chick-a-dee-dee-dee* call are familiar year-round. The chickadee is friendly and sociable, easily tamed and even hand-fed.

Description

Both sexes measure 5 inches, colored grayish above and pale below, with a bold black cap and bib, white cheeks, and white bars on black wings. In the southwest, the black-capped is replaced by the Carolina chickadee.

Preferred Habitat

Chickadees nest in tree cavities or simple bird boxes in gardens, mixed and deciduous forests, and residential areas.

Feeding Habits

Traveling in small feeding flocks, the birds work together to locate plentiful food sources, particularly in winter. They glean insects and larvae from branches and foliage, as well as seeds and berries.

Migration Habits

Across most of the northern United States from the Upper Midwest to the Pacific Northwest chickadees are year-round residents. In autumn they join small mixed flocks of titmice, nuthatches, kinglets, creepers, and warblers to roost and forage together during the harsh winter months.

Placement of Feeders

Seed and suet feeders attract these cheery backyard visitors, and they are usually one of the first birds to find and inhabit a new nesting box.

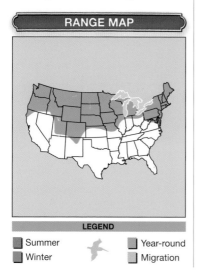

RANGE MAP

LEGEND

Summer

Winter

Year-round

Migration

Black-crowned Night Heron

As its name suggests, this heron is most active at night, but can often be seen during daylight feeding along edges of lakes and lagoons or roosting in trees. At sundown, when most herons return to the nest, these birds leave their roosts and set out to hunt.

Description

Hunched and stocky, the night heron measures 22-28 inches. Adults have a black cap and back, red eyes, gray wings, yellow legs, and a white belly. Streaky gray juveniles closely resemble the American bittern.

Preferred Habitat

In marshes, rivers, or wooded swamps, this heron piles up a mass of sticks to craft a messy platform nest. These fragile constructions are often disrupted by storms or high winds, dumping the chicks unceremoniously on the rubble below the rookery.

Feeding Habits

Silent and menacing, the heron perches on the edge of a pond or marsh waiting for its aquatic prey—frogs, fish, and crustaceans—to chance within range.

Migration Habits

This heron summers throughout almost all states and remains year-round along the Pacific, Gulf, and Atlantic Coasts.

Placement of Feeders

Its scientific name, *nycticorax*, means "night raven." Listen for this bird's loud, barking *squawk*, a common nighttime sound.

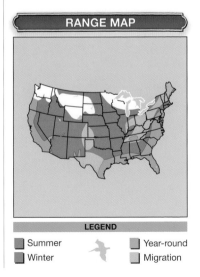

RANGE MAP

LEGEND

- Summer
- Winter
- Year-round
- Migration

black

Weighing only half an ounce, the 6-inch blackpoll warbler is America's only small land bird to make the transoceanic journey of 10,000 miles between northern Canada and the rainforests of northeast South America, crossing vast stretches of the Atlantic Ocean and Gulf of Mexico.

Description

Breeding males are streaked black and white, with a black crown and throat and white cheeks. Females, juveniles, and nonbreeding males are greenish with pale legs.

Preferred Habitat

In the spruce forests of Canada's Far North, these hardy birds craft a secure cup of twigs, stems, and grass in a spruce or fir tree, lining the nest with feathers to keep the fledglings warm.

Feeding Habits

Gleaning from foliage or flycatching, the blackpoll consumes caterpillars, spiders, wasps, aphids, mosquitoes, and other insects. In their wintering grounds, the warblers subsist on nectar, fruit, and pollen.

Migration Habits

Crossing thousands of miles each spring and autumn, the blackpoll warbler faces many dangers. They rest and feed by day and migrate at night, often crashing head-on into tall buildings, TV towers, and lighthouses.

Placement of Feeders

The blackpolls are very late migrants through the United States, commonly resting and feeding in oak forests.

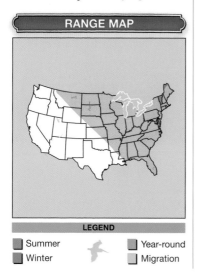

RANGE MAP

LEGEND

■ Summer ■ Year-round
■ Winter ■ Migration

black

the young are fledged before harvest time, or in conifers.

Feeding Habits
A year-round diet of insects and seeds is supplemented in autumn when Brewer's blackbirds swarm granaries and farms to feast on spilled grain.

Migration Habits
In summer these birds breed in small colonies, but when the fledglings can fly, they join up with neighboring colonies and flocks of red-wings, cowbirds, starlings, and grackles to form a migratory mob of tens of thousands of birds.

Placement of Feeders
Scatter seed or grain on the ground for these blackbirds to peck at.

N amed by John J. Audubon for the nineteenth-century ornithologist Thomas M. Brewer, this blackbird happily makes its home among humans in urban developments. As it trots along the ground, its head jerks back and forth like a chicken's.

Description
The male is solid black, up to 10 inches long, with a glossy purple-blue head. The female is dull gray with dark eyes. An excited blackbird makes an array of gurgles, squawks, and whistles, while its creaking song is *k-shee*.

Preferred Habitat
Open country, farmyards, parks, and lawns provide ample food and ideal nesting conditions. Colonies of up to 30 pairs may nest in hay fields, where

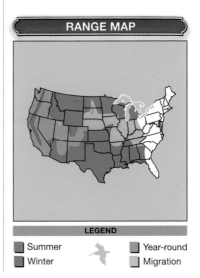

RANGE MAP

LEGEND

Summer — Year-round
Winter — Migration

This perky species is very similar to the black-capped chickadee, but their ranges replace each other geographically. Its four-syllable *phee-bee, phee-bay* whistle is twice as long as the black-cap's song.

Description

At only 4.5 inches the Carolina chickadee is one of the smallest in its family. The handsome bird is gray above and pale buff below, with a black cap and bib, and white cheeks.

Preferred Habitat

These chickadees are woodland birds, residing in deciduous, mixed, and coniferous forest, wooded swamps, gardens, and parks. In a tree cavity or birdhouse the chickadee crafts a cup-shaped nest of moss, plants, and feathers.

Feeding Habits

Insects make up about half of the chickadee's diet, supplemented by berries and seeds from shrubs, pines, and weeds. Usually traveling in pairs or small groups, chickadees swiftly communicate each flock member's successful foraging location or strategy.

Migration Habits

These birds are a common permanent resident from Texas north to New Jersey. In autumn, they join up with mixed flocks of kinglets, creepers, warblers, titmice, and nuthatches.

Placement of Feeders

Backyards with sufficient trees and shrubbery are often host to the cheery chickadee, who readily visits seed feeders with its mixed flock.

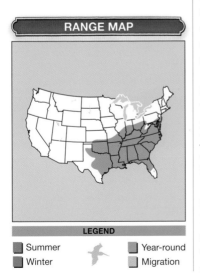

RANGE MAP

LEGEND

- Summer
- Winter
- Year-round
- Migration

black

Cliff Swallow

Signaling the coming spring with its appearance at California's Capistrano Mission each year, the cliff swallow is known for its elaborate gourd-shaped nests, constructed out of mud on the sides of barns, buildings, or the rocky cliffs for which it is named.

Description
Distinct from the barn swallow for its square tail and pointed wings, this 6-inch swallow is blue-black on top with a white forehead and a rust-colored throat and rump.

Preferred Habitat
Open country with a fresh water source and nearby barns or buildings for nesting is the ideal environment for this bird. Unfortunately, the introduction of the house sparrow, which forces cliff swallows out of nesting sites, has reduced their population considerably.

Feeding Habits
Like other swallows, these birds snatch flying insects and airborne spiders in flight, and may dip down to drink from the surface of rivers or lakes.

Migration Habits
Widespread in North America in summer, the cliff swallow migrates southward in flocks of hundreds come autumn. They return faithfully to the same nesting sites annually, nesting in huge colonies.

Placement of Feeders
Thousands of breeding pairs have been known to nest in a single barn, but be grateful for the innumerable insects they will consume.

RANGE MAP

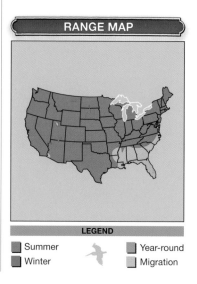

LEGEND

Summer

Winter

Year-round

Migration

black

Downies are the smallest and friendliest of the North American woodpeckers. Like their tree-hammering relatives, a strong bill, neck, and reinforced skull protect the brain from repeated hammering, and bristly feathers protect the nostrils.

Description

This species is a 7-inch version of the hairy woodpecker. The back and belly are white, the black wings spotted white, and the tail barred. Males have a red patch on the head, and both have a thin black mustache.

Preferred Habitat

Any urban or rural area with deciduous trees can be home to this small woodpecker. Mating pairs excavate a cavity in a tree, stump, or fence post to build the nest. Parents share incubation

and feeding duties.

Feeding Habits

Foraging among foliage and under bark with its sharply barbed tongue, the bird consumes insects, larvae, and grubs. In winter they can be found consuming dormant wasps and corn-borers.

Migration Habits

The downy is found in almost all of North America, remaining in the North all winter to forage with chickadees and kinglets among frozen fields and backyards.

Placement of Feeders

Feeding stations featuring berries, beef suet, peanut butter, pecans, or sunflower seeds will be home to plucky downies, especially in winter.

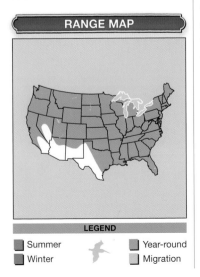

RANGE MAP

LEGEND

Summer

Winter

Year-round

Migration

black

Feeding Habits

For most of the year its diet consists entirely of flying insects, but in winter it subsists on the fruit and berries of poison ivy and poison sumac, and may even scoop little fish from shallow water.

Migration Habits

This hardy flycatcher has a long breeding season in the East, but spends the summer months from northern Texas through the Midwest, in to the entire New England area.

Placement of Feeders

Although tame and common in suburbs and farmland, the eastern phoebe rarely visits feeding stations. The best field mark is the constant downward "wagging" of its long tail.

From its perch on a dead branch, an unremarkable 7-inch bird sweetly chants *fee-bee* over and over. Suddenly a flying insect catches its eye, and it darts out to snatch it, returning swiftly to its favorite perch.

Description

This phoebe is best distinguished from other flycatchers by its lack of wing bars or eye ring. It is gray-brown or olive above and white below, with a black bill.

Preferred Habitat

Phoebes prefer to live near a freshwater source but are well adapted to living among human developments. They attach mud nests to vertical walls, barn rafters, windowsills, and bridge supports. Hard-working females raise two broods each season.

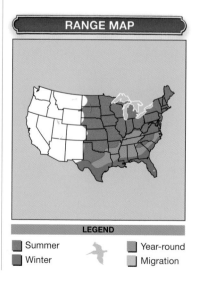

RANGE MAP

LEGEND

Summer | Year-round
Winter | Migration

In 1890 a Shakespeare enthusiast released 100 starlings in New York City in an effort to introduce all feathered friends mentioned in Shakespeare's works. Now numbering 200 million, starlings are noisy and messy, but they consume a large quantity of insects.

Description

Shiny black with a green or purple sheen in summer, the bird molts in autumn, growing a winter coat of white-speckled feathers. The stout, 7.5-inch starling is a skillful imitator known for its wolf-whistle call.

Preferred Habitat

Especially common around landfills or grain elevators, the starling is at home in cities, suburbs, or farmland. The female constructs a nest of twigs and trash in a tree or cavity.

Feeding Habits

City dwellers and rural residents alike can spot these birds probing for insects, spiders, worms, fruit, grain, or seeds from parks to farmyards.

Migration Habits

This native of Eurasia is found year-round across the entire United States. During colder months they fly in enormous swarms to roost in warmer downtown areas.

Placement of Feeders

Starlings are drawn to seed and suet feeders, but if you intend your nest boxes for native species such as bluebirds, woodpeckers, or purple martins, monitor them carefully for starling habitation.

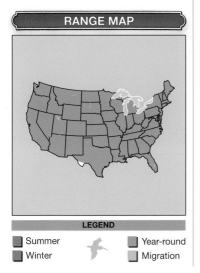

RANGE MAP

LEGEND

- Summer
- Winter
- Year-round
- Migration

black

Woodpeckers are not known for vocalization, and despite their sharp *peek* call, the birds prefer to regale each other with a drumming "song" made by jackhammering dead tree trunks with their stout bills.

Description

Larger than the similar downy woodpecker, the 9-inch hairy species is mainly black above, with white-spotted wings and a white back, and white below. The head has a black crown, stripes on the face, and small red patches. Juveniles are brown.

Preferred Habitat

This shy forest bird is found in mixed and coniferous forests, wooded swamps, and river bottoms. In the spring parent birds busily excavate a cavity in a tree or shrub to house their eggs.

Feeding Habits

Using its sturdy tail like a tripod, this woodpecker hammers into tree trunks and shreds strips of bark to excavate wood-boring insects, bark beetles, ants, and spiders, or the occasional hazelnut or acorn.

Migration Habits

Regardless of the season or weather conditions, this bird can be found in all states, cheerily chipping away loose tree bark.

Placement of Feeders

The hairy woodpecker is not so common a backyard visitor as the downy, but it is drawn to raw apples, bananas, peanut butter, and sunflower seeds, and it is especially fond of beef suet.

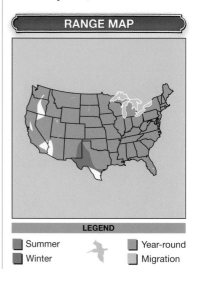

RANGE MAP

LEGEND

| Summer | Year-round |
| Winter | Migration |

Tiny but hardy, the pipit nests only in the harsh tundra environment. American birders are likely to see them during migration, where they rest in mud flats and wet grain fields, though nesting pairs do appear throughout the Rocky Mountain range.

Description
Breeding birds, at 5–7 inches long, are grayish above and buff below with a white-rimmed tail. Autumn birds are streaky gray-brown above and heavily streaked white below. The thin legs and beak are dark.

Preferred Habitat
Males establish nesting territories on alpine or Arctic tundra before the snow melts, ready for a quick breeding season. During nonbreeding season

they can be found on dunes, plowed fields, and shores.

Feeding Habits
Walking slowly on sturdy legs, the pipit consumes insects, spiders, snails, mayflies, and dragonflies and their larvae. In winter it eats mainly seeds.

Migration Habits
In March males head to their breeding range in the Rocky Mountains, while females follow in May. In September, flocks head south to the southern United States.

Placement of Feeders
The pipit seldom stops to perch, but listen for its quick *pipit* call in flight and observe its constant tail-bobbing action.

RANGE MAP

LEGEND
- Summer
- Winter
- Year-round
- Migration

gray

American Robin

As the herald of spring in northern states, the robin's chipper call of *cheerily cheer up cheerio* pierces the early morning stillness. Although technically a thrush—and the only widespread thrush in America—the bird is named for its resemblance to the redbreasted robin of Europe.

Description
The male, at 9–11 inches long, is gray on top, with a black head and bright red breast. The female is similar in appearance but duller, with a gray head.

Preferred Habitat
Lawns, gardens, parks, forests, and farmland are favorite locations, but birds that winter in the northern states may roost in cedar bogs and swamps.

Feeding Habits
As it hops across a lawn with its head cocked, the robin is hunting for insects and earthworms. Berries provide sustenance through the winter.

Migration Habits
Though not all robins head south for the winter, each year huge flocks of up to 300,000 birds head northward in spring, with each bird returning to the area of his birth. Summer is spent in select regions, one being the Upper Midwest.

Placement of Feeders
While not regular visitors to feeders, they may be drawn to mealworms, bread, raisins, or fruit. They are easily sighted on a grassy lawn rooting for worms, and may build nests on ledges or windowsills.

RANGE MAP

LEGEND

■ Summer ■ Year-round
■ Winter ■ Migration

P iercing the night with a spine-tingling hiss and scream, the barn owl pursues an evening meal of mice or rabbits. This owl species is tolerant of human presence, often making its home in barns.

Description

The barn owl, at 13–19 inches long, is easily recognized by its long legs, dark eyes, and heart-shaped face. Colored golden brown with a greyish hue above and white below, it appears pure white in flight.

Preferred Habitat

A widespread species, the barn owl is found on six of seven continents, where it inhabits grasslands, marshes, deserts, and residential and urban areas.

Feeding Habits

Garbage dumps, cemeteries, and farms are favorite hunting grounds for rodents, small mammals, or other birds. The owl has good daytime eyesight, but can track its prey by sound alone in complete darkness.

Migration Habits

The barn owl inhabits almost all states year-round, laying eggs in buildings, hollow trees, caves, or burrows. They also practice population control, producing few or no eggs when food is scarce.

Placement of Feeders

These nocturnal hunters can be seen soaring alongside highways or rural roads at dusk as they scan the ground for prey, and they may select a local barn or bell tower for nesting.

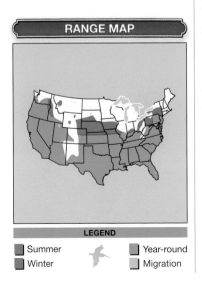

RANGE MAP

LEGEND

■ Summer ■ Year-round
■ Winter ■ Migration

gray

Feeding Habits

Hovering over the water, a flash of blue spirals into a deadly dive, clutching a stunned fish back to its perch, where it beats the fish and swallows it whole. Bones and scales are later regurgitated as pellets. Favorite foods include fish, tadpoles, salamanders, frogs, insects, crabs, or crayfish. Young are taught to retrieve dead fish from the water.

Migration Habits

Found year-round throughout most of the nation, this fierce fisher travels to the northern border states during summer only.

Placement of Feeders

Patient observation along the water's edge will reveal favorite perches and may allow you to witness their diving spectacle.

A long a quiet river bank, a large blue-gray bird with a ragged crest issues a rattling *crick-crick-crick* from a nearby perch. The kingfisher is an aggressive, independent hunter.

Description

Pigeon-sized at 11–14 inches long, this crested bird is blue-gray above with a crest and white collar. The male has a blue-gray band across the chest, while the female has two chest bands and brighter coloring.

Preferred Habitat

These fish-eaters never stray far from water. The mating pair tunnels into the bank alongside a favorite river or lake, where the female lays eggs in the cool, dark burrow.

gray

RANGE MAP

LEGEND

■ Summer ■ Year-round
■ Winter ■ Migration

Common Redpoll

This Arctic finch of northern Canada survives colder temperatures more than any other songbird. Sociable and nonterritorial even in nesting season, redpolls travel in flocks that irregularly visit the northern states during winter.

Description

The best field marks of the 5-inch redpoll are its raspberry-red cap and black chin. Adults are streaky gray-brown above with a white belly, and males have red on the chest and rump.

Preferred Habitat

Breeding in Arctic tundra, birch groves, and northern coniferous forest, the female builds a small, heavily insulated nest on a platform of twigs. In winter flocks are found in brushy or weedy fields and thickets.

Feeding Habits

To meet its energy needs the bird eats constantly, foraging on the ground for seeds of pine, hemlock, birch, and alder, various grass seeds, and buds of trees and shrubs. The bird also has a special pouch in its esophagus for delayed digesting.

Migration Habits

Generally redpolls live year-round in Canada, but in harsh winters large flocks wander southward in search of warmer climates. Some have been spotted as far south as Nebraska and as far west as Washington.

Placement of Feeders

In mixed flocks of goldfinches and siskins, the tame redpoll readily visits backyard feeders for niger and sunflower seeds.

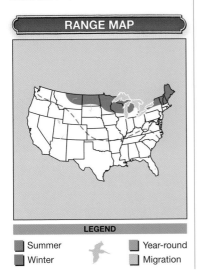

RANGE MAP

LEGEND

- Summer
- Winter
- Year-round
- Migration

gray

Cooper's Hawk

Once known as the "chicken hawk" for its preference for barnyard fowl, this large hawk was hunted by the thousands, and many other hawk species suffered the same fate. Populations also diminished temporarily with the use of DDT.

Description
This species is almost identical to the sharp-shinned hawk, but larger and more powerful at 15–20 inches long. Adults are dark blue-gray above and white-barred red below, with a dark cap. Juveniles are streaked with brown.

Preferred Habitat
Open deciduous forests and mixed woodlands are traditional habitats of Cooper's hawks, but they are increasingly common in urban and suburban yards. In their high platform nest of sticks, the male feeds the incubating female, and she feeds the chicks.

Feeding Habits
The large hawk is easily outmaneuvered by songbirds, but it relies on surprise and speed to catch birds, squirrels, and chipmunks. It may return with its captured meal to a feeding roost.

Migration Habits
The species is found year-round in almost all states except the Great Plains, breeding slightly north and summering in the Upper Midwest.

Placement of Feeders
These woodland birds are best identified as they glide overhead by their rounded wings and long, rounded tail.

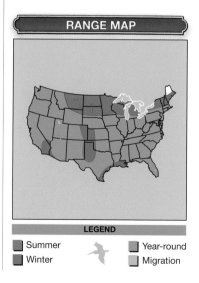

RANGE MAP

LEGEND
Summer
Winter
Year-round
Migration

gray

The dark-eyed species consolidates what were formerly thought to be up to five different species: the slate-colored, Oregon, white-winged, pink-sided, and gray-headed juncos. But despite their varied coloring, these birds breed freely with each other, and all issue a similar, slow, musical trill.

Description

All measuring 5–6.5 inches long, with a pinkish bill and dark eyes, there are distinct plumage variations. The eastern slate bird is gray above and below; the gray-head of the southern Rockies is rust or brown above; the pink-sided junco of the Central Rockies has pinkish marks on its sides; the Oregon variety has a black head and brown back, while the white-winged version of the Black Hills has white wing bars and tail.

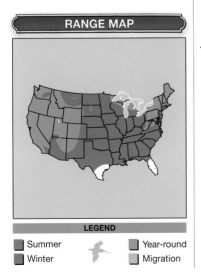

RANGE MAP

LEGEND

- ▮ Summer
- ▮ Winter
- ▮ Year-round
- ▮ Migration

Preferred Habitat

Juncos live in open woodlands and clearings throughout North America.

Feeding Habits

With a unique double-scratching motion, juncos dig for insects. They also enjoy seeds and berries.

Migration Habits

Found throughout the continental United States in the winter and migrating north in summer, the junco nests on the ground and maintains a rigid flock hierarchy. It can be found year-round throughout the western third of the United States.

gray

Placement of Feeders

This frequent feeder visitor prefers millet, sunflower hearts, and finely cracked corn from low platform feeders.

Feeding Habits

Hunting at night on silent wings, the owl scoops up rodents, birds, earthworms, and snakes with its deadly talons. It can also catch insects on the wing or plunge into streams to snatch fish.

Migration Habits

The eastern screech owl is a year-round resident east of the Rockies, but on rare occasion has been spotted as far west as the mountains of Montana.

Placement of Feeders

Birders may never detect the owl's nighttime visits to backyard birdbaths, but the elusive guest sometimes uses nest boxes. Listen for their loud horse-whinny calls after dark.

Two distinct colorings define this small owl—rusty red or mottled gray-brown. Unaffected by season, sex, or age, each bird's permanent coloring varies by relative population in a given habitat.

Description

Identified by its distinctive ear tufts, fixed yellow eyes, and white wing spots, the 10-inch red or gray owl gives a variety of chilling calls, including screeching, purring, trilling, and a descending wail.

Preferred Habitat

The eastern species prefers mature deciduous forest, lakeshores, orchards, or open forest, as well as suburban areas. The female lays eggs in a tree—especially small red cedars—or nest box.

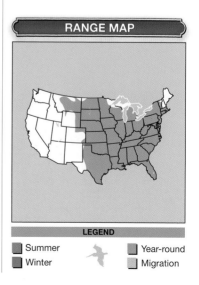

RANGE MAP

LEGEND

Summer

Winter

Year-round

Migration

Second only to the mockingbird for its impressive mimicry, the male catbird, with a special ability to sing two notes at once, fills the air with a medley of area birdcalls, shrieks, whistles, and its notorious cat-like whine.

Description

Long and thin, the catbird measures 8–9.75 inches, colored dark gray above with a black cap, and a dark rust patch on its rump.

Preferred Habitat

The catbird is at home in thickets, brush, and gardens, where it raises two broods each season in a tangle of vines or shrubs. Though tolerant of certain species, the gray catbird is territorial and may pierce the eggs of other songbirds, including cowbird eggs found in its own nest.

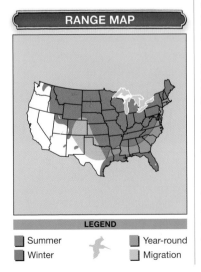

RANGE MAP

LEGEND

■ Summer
■ Winter
■ Year-round
■ Migration

Feeding Habits

Ants, beetles, moths, grasshoppers, dragonflies, and spiders are found by foraging on the ground and in shrubs, while berries of the dogwood, mulberry, elderberry, and wild grape trees round out the catbird's diet.

Migration Habits

In summer, the catbird breeds across most of the continent, while it winters along the Gulf Coast. These nighttime migrators often collide with aerial antennae and TV towers.

Placement of Feeders

This boisterous garden visitor may take up residence in a tangle of shrubs or briars alongside a house and is fond of birdbaths.

gray

Feeding Habits

Clinging to a branch, the titmouse swings upside down to pluck spiders and insects from the underside of foliage. Acorn masts and oak galls are favorites in autumn, as well as fruit and seeds.

Migration Habits

For most of the year these birds travel in pairs, but in autumn they join with small flocks of chickadees, kinglets, and nuthatches for social foraging. From Nebraska eastward they are common year-round.

Placement of Feeders

Beechnuts, acorns, and shelled peanuts score big with these noisy, friendly backyard visitors, and mating pairs that select a nesting box on your property will stay all year.

B reeding season makes titmice anxious and irritable, and they are notorious for pulling hair from sleeping dogs, cats, and livestock to line their nests. But their cheery, ringing *peter, peter, peter!* charms at the winter feeder.

Description

Sparrow-sized at 6.5 inches, the crested bird is gray above, whitish below, with buff flanks and rusty sides. Those in Texas and Oklahoma have a black crest.

Preferred Habitat

Mating pairs seek bottomlands and wet forests, raising their brood in a hole in a mature oak tree. In autumn they roam deciduous forests with a mixed flock, frequenting gardens and parks.

RANGE MAP

LEGEND

Summer — Year-round
Winter — Migration

gray

An extra long hind toe claw allows the nuthatch to creep down tree trunks headfirst. Like its red-breasted relative, the white-breasted nuthatch gives a low-pitched *yank-yank* call and a low whistled song, including a *whi-whi-whi-whi* mating song.

Description

Larger than the red-breast, this bird measures 5–6 inches, colored blue-gray above with a black crown and white underparts. Its black eye is conspicuous in a white face.

Preferred Habitat

Mating pairs remain together year-round, usually in dry oak or pine oak forests or other deciduous forests. Adult birds nest in a natural cavity or bird box, or excavate a new hole.

Feeding Habits

Using its long, thin bill, the nuthatch forages under loose bark and in tree crevices for insects and larvae.

Migration Habits

Nuthatches are found year-round in almost all continental states. Occasionally they migrate to the outer coasts but are usually sedentary. In winter nuthatches join flocks of chickadees, woodpeckers, and kinglets to roam for food within their territories.

Placement of Feeders

Seed feeders and suet cakes draw these familiar winter visitors to backyard feeders. They are cheery and friendly, though not tame, and will use available nest boxes.

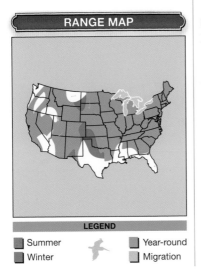

RANGE MAP

LEGEND

Summer

Winter

Year-round

Migration

white

Among white-throated sparrows, two coloring variations occur—white head stripes or tan head stripes—and birds tend to choose mating pairs with the opposite coloring. Their clear, whistled song has been transcribed in several ways, but *sweet, sweet Canada, Canada, Canada* is a common translation.

Description

The sexes look the same, measuring 6–7 inches long, streaked brown above and buff or gray below. Both have a conspicuous white throat patch, a dark bill, and yellow patches between the eyes.

Preferred Habitat

Brushy undergrowth in coniferous forests is the sparrow's preferred breeding ground, where it builds a nest of grass and moss on or near the ground under small trees. In winter, they are found in brushy areas, pastures, bogs, and suburbs.

Feeding Habits

The sparrow captures insects by scratching on the ground, scouring vegetation, or flycatching. Weed seeds and the fruit of dogwood, sumac, and elderberry trees are also favorites.

Migration Habits

Best known in the United States as a winter visitor, they reside across most of the East and Midwest and along the West Coast, with a breeding range in the North.

Placement of Feeders

In cold months, backyard bushes may be filled with roosting white-throats. They are drawn to feeders offering cracked corn or seeds.

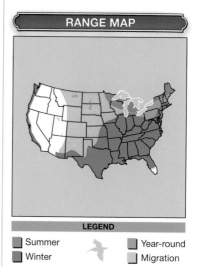

RANGE MAP

LEGEND

Summer   Year-round
Winter   Migration

white

INDEX

INDEX